Nino's Last

The final opinions of
Justice Antonin Scalia

A collection of Justice Scalia's
SCOTUS opinions from the 2015 term.

collected by

JOSHUA WARREN

DEDICATION

to Italian American jurisprudence.

"The seed is the word"

~ Luke 8:11, quoted on the podium at the Basilica of the National Shrine of the Immaculate Conception during Scalia's funeral, February 20, 2016.

ACKNOWLEDGMENT

This book would not be possible without
the continuing support and encouragement of my family.

Thank you to everyone who supports unreasonable logic.

EDITOR'S NOTE

The following is a collection of the final orders and opinions written by U.S. Supreme Court Associate Justice Antonin Scalia during the 2015 term leading up to his death on February 13, 2016. At that time the court was composed of Chief Justice Roberts and Associate Justices Scalia, Kennedy, Thomas, Ginsburg, Breyer, Alito, Sotomayor, and Kagan.

This book includes six opinions in total. These are the only opinions decided in the 2015 term for which Scalia has the opportunity to file an opinion. Presumably he had many more recent draft opinions written in his last weeks. This book is only his last public legal opinions.

For these six case decisions, only the opinions written by Justice Scalia are included. The page numbers are omitted but citations to the Supreme Court reporter series are provided. This book includes two majority opinions (one unanimous and one 8-1 decision with Justice Sotomayor dissenting), one concurring opinion (to a Kennedy majority), and three dissenting opinions (two joined by both Justices Alito and Thomas, and one joined only by Justice Thomas). Also, one of the dissents is from a denial of petition for certiorari. This variation in such a short set provides a good introduction to the format of Supreme Court opinions for new legal readers. Ample additional information about each of these cases is readily available by internet search.

The cases are presented in chronological order. Both *FERC v EPSA* and *Montgomery v. Louisiana* were decided on January 25, 2016. *FERC* was reported later so it concludes this book. However, had *Montgomery* been printed last, the Justice's final words would have been "Mission Accomplished." Instead, *FERC*'s final words are also fitting for this Justice: "I respectfully dissent."

FOREWORD

What is a majority opinion?

The Supreme Court of the United State is composed of nine justices. This court is the highest appellate court in the United States federal jurisdiction. Decisions of the court are by the majority decision of the nine justices. If at least five justices are willing to sign an opinion then the holding becomes law. The holding is the outcome of the case as for that particular case, with those particular facts. The holding becomes law to be used by the lower courts to apply the law consistent with the principles of stare decisis. In order to apply the holding properly the lower courts need to understand the holding and so the majority opinion is the explanation of the court's reasoning.

What is a concurring opinion?

Sometimes, a judge agrees with the holding as to the particular case but disagrees about the reasons why the holding is correct. In this case, the judge would write a concurring opinion. Often, the majority opinion is largely dicta, expressions of rationale that are not directly related to the specific facts of the case. The reasoning of the majority opinion must be applied at the lower courts. However, because there is no higher court than the Supreme Court of the United State, the reasoning of the majority opinion of this court is only as strong as the lifespan of the justices' jurisprudential consistency and the duration of their tenure on the court.

What is a dissenting opinion?

Like a concurring opinion, the dissenting opinion is not law. It is the non-majority opinion of a judge, sometimes filed alone, sometimes joined by other judges. In the case of the Supreme Court, these are very important judges and so the dissents become useful for predicting future cases. Understanding the opinions of Supreme Court dissents is useful for understanding the way that these important people think about the law.

Does it make sense to read a justice's dissenting or concurring opinion, or any dicta, out of context without reading the majority opinion too?

If you find any of these Scalia opinions interesting, go read more about that case on the internet. More information about each of these cases is easily found on the internet, consider using supremecourt.gov, scotusblog.com, oyez.org, law.cornell.edu, as well as Wikipedia.org, and search engines, like Google (and Google Scholar), to find more information about any of these cases.

Does it make sense for any non-lawyers to read Supreme Court opinions?

It can be hard work to read court opinions but imagine how difficult it is to write one. Often the public thinks the act of being a Supreme Court judge is simply to decide which side of the issue they like better. The work of weaving reasoned arguments from textual sources is hard work. The general public should have more exposure to the workings within the public decision-making processes. In American democracy, the law is the responsibility of all citizens, not just the lawyers, and the first step to becoming involved in the law is to learn to read it.

INTRODUCTION TO READING COURT OPINIONS FOR FUN
(and learning)

THE ONLY RULE is PATIENCE

If you are reading this then you already know how to read. Go somewhere with appropriate lighting and a comfortable chair and read patiently. Mark unusual words and move on. Later use a legal dictionary and internet search engines to amplify your understanding. With patience you will learn to read better.

As you begin to read a case, notice the year and consider world historical conditions of that time. In this book, all of these opinions are decisions from the 2015 term of the U.S. Supreme Court. In all of these cases there was previous action in the lower courts. Identify the parties, what they were seeking from the court, and what prior legal actions have already occurred.

Or just jump right in at any paragraph you like and start reading. This book is designed to read Justice Scalia's final court writings. There is no overreaching legal thesis and the cases are not individually summarized. These real court opinions are arranged chronologically with hopes of sparking interest in reading Justice Scalia's writing and legal writing in general.

Reading law will improve your ability to read law.

As you read you may consider yourself as a law clerk and try to summarize the arguments and holdings of each case. This is good practice and any attempt to write (and re-write) a case summary will promote your thinking. But if you prefer, just sit under a tree and enjoy the writings of a Supreme Court justice.

These are all serious legal texts each with a serious legal purpose but they are also appreciable as the high art of American legal civilization. This collection is gathered with the hope of finding enjoyment in these works of art from one of America's top jurisprudential writers.

INTRODUCTION TO NINO'S LAST

Justice Scalia was a judicial force. Born to Italian immigrants from Sicily, Scalia was raised in Queens, NY. In 1960 he graduated magna cum laude from Harvard Law School. He became associate justice of the U.S. Supreme Court in 1986. He was nominated by President Ronald Reagan to fill the seat vacated by Justice Rehnquist upon the latter's promotion to chief justice. Scalia was confirmed by a Senate vote of 98-0 but would become a polarizing figure on the court.

Antonin Scalia, called Nino by his friends, was a devout Roman Catholic. He was the first Italian American to sit on America's highest court. He was also known for his originalist philosophy and support of State's legislative rights generally. He was a strong supporter of the rights of the 2nd amendment against the federal government, and the State's right to impose the death penalty. He was known for his opposition to a woman's right to choose abortion, and more recently, his opposition to the application of equal protection to same-sex marriage.

Regardless of his positions on the issues, Justice Scalia will be remembered for his writing style. His conversational writing and prolific production of consumer media publication made him an iconic figure in the modern media era. His interpretations of original intent have shaped constitutional debates for nearly three decades.

He reserved some of his most caustic wit for near the end. In the final days of the 2014 Term he signed dissents in King v. Burwell (about Obamacare) and Obergefell v. Hodges (about same-sex marriage) in which he referred to the his colleagues' majority opinions as "jiggery-pokery" and "pure applesauce".

It was not uncommon for Justice Scalia to be joined by Justice Thomas and more recently in trio with Justice Alito. Still, a careful reader will not overemphasize their common coalition. The jurisprudential ideas of each justice, and particularly the great justices, are unique and the fault lines between them are often surprising.

The only way to understand the jurisprudence of any particular Supreme Court is to read the justices' opinions. This book is provided for a historical perspective Justice Scalia's reasoning at the end of his tenure. These are Justice Scalia's last opinions. May that he rest in peace.

Nino's Last

CHRONOLOGICAL TABLE OF AUTHORITY

Mullenix v. Luna

Supreme Court of the United States
November 9, 2015, Decided
No. 14-1143.
136 S. Ct. 305

CHADRIN LEE MULLENIX,
PETITIONER
v.
BEATRICE LUNA,
INDIVIDUALLY
AND AS
REPRESENTATIVE OF THE ESTATE OF
ISRAEL LEIJA, JR., ET AL.

Petition for writ of certiorari to the United States Court of Appeals for the Fifth Circuit granted and decision summarily reversed.

8-1 Decision; 1 Concurrence; 1 Dissent.

Reversed.

JUSTICE SCALIA, concurring in the judgment.

I join the judgment of the Court, but would not describe what occurred here as the application of deadly force in effecting an arrest. Our prior cases have reserved that description to the directing of force sufficient to kill *at the person* of the desired arrestee. See, *e.g.*, *Plumhoff v. Rickard,* 572 U.S. ___, 134 S. Ct. 2012, 188 L. Ed. 2d 1056, 1061 (2014); *Brosseau v. Haugen,* 543 U.S. 194, 125 S. Ct. 596, 160 L. Ed. 2d 583 (2004) (*per curiam*); *Tennessee v. Garner,* 471 U.S. 1, 105 S. Ct. 1694, 85 L. Ed. 2d 1 (1985). It does not assist analysis to refer to all use of force that happens to kill the arrestee as the application of deadly force. The police might, for example, attempt to stop a fleeing felon's car by felling a large tree across the road; if they drop the tree too late, so that it crushes the car and its occupant, I would not call that the application of deadly force. Though it was force sufficient to kill, it was not applied with the object of harming the body of the felon.

Thus, in *Scott v. Harris,* 550 U.S. 372, 127 S. Ct. 1769, 167 L. Ed. 2d 686 (2007), we declined to characterize officer Scott's use of his pursuing vehicle's bumper to push the fleeing vehicle off the road as the application of deadly force. Whether or not it was that, we said, "all that matters is whether Scott's actions were reasonable." *Id., at 383, 127 S. Ct. 1769, 167 L. Ed. 2d 686.* So also here. But it stacks the deck against the officer, it seems to me, to describe his action as the application of deadly force.

It was at least arguable in *Scott* that pushing a speeding vehicle off the road is targeting its occupant for injury or death. Here, however, it is conceded that Trooper Mullenix did not shoot to wound or kill the fleeing Leija, nor even to drive Leija's car off the road, but only to cause the car to stop by destroying its engine. That was a risky enterprise, as the outcome demonstrated; but determining whether it violated the *Fourth Amendment* requires us to ask, not whether it was reasonable to kill Leija, but whether it was reasonable to shoot at the engine in light of the risk to Leija. It distorts that inquiry, I think, to make the question whether it was reasonable for Mullenix to "apply deadly force."

Rapelje v. Blackston

Supreme Court of the United States
November 30, 2015, Decided
No. 15-161.
136 S. Ct. 388

LLOYD RAPELJE,
WARDEN
v.
JUNIOR FRED BLACKSTON

Petition for writ of certiorari to the United States Court of Appeals for the Sixth Circuit denied.

Denied.

JUSTICE SCALIA, with whom JUSTICE THOMAS and JUSTICE ALITO join, dissenting from denial of certiorari.

A criminal defendant "shall enjoy the right . . . to be confronted with the witnesses against him." *U. S. Const., Amdt. 6.* We have held that this right entitles the accused to cross-examine witnesses who testify at trial, and to exclude certain out-of-court statements that the defendant did not have a prior opportunity to cross-examine. *Crawford v. Washington, 541 U. S. 36, 50-51, 124 S. Ct. 1354, 158 L. Ed. 2d 177 (2004); Davis v. Alaska, 415 U. S. 308, 315-317, 94 S. Ct. 1105, 39 L. Ed. 2d 347 (1974).* We have never held — nor would the verb "to confront" support the holding — that confrontation includes the right to *admit* out-of-court statements into evidence. Nevertheless, the Sixth Circuit held not only that the *Confrontation Clause* guarantees the right to admit such evidence but that our cases have "clearly established" as much. We should grant certiorari and summarily reverse.

Respondent Junior Fred Blackston was convicted in Michigan state court of first-degree murder on the strength of the testimony of five people, some of whom participated in the crime. For reasons not relevant here, the court ordered a new trial. Before Blackston's retrial, however, two of the five witnesses signed written statements recanting their trial testimony. The prosecution called them at the second trial, but they refused to answer any questions. The trial court therefore pronounced them "unavailable" and, pursuant to a venerable hearsay exception, see *Mich. Rule Evid. 804(b)(1)* (2012); cf. 5 J. Wigmore, Evidence §1370, p. 55 (J. Chadbourn rev. 1974), allowed their earlier testimony to be read to the jury. But the court refused to admit into evidence their written recantations.

Blackston was once again convicted of first-degree murder and sentenced to life imprisonment. Affirming the conviction, the Supreme Court of Michigan held that the trial court's exclusion of the recantations was not error and, even if it was, was harmless beyond a reasonable doubt. *481 Mich. 451, 751 N. W. 2d 408 (2008).*

This petition for federal habeas relief followed. The District Court conditionally granted the writ, finding that the exclusion of the recantations violated Blackston's *Sixth* and *Fourteenth Amendment* rights. *907 F. Supp. 2d 878 (ED Mich. 2012).* A divided Sixth Circuit panel affirmed. *780 F. 3d 340 (2015).* In the Court of Appeals' view, "[t]here is a clearly established right to impeach the credibility of an adverse witness using the witness's own inconsistent statements." *Id., at 348.* The recantations, reasoned the court, were inconsistent statements that had obvious impeachment value.

The Antiterrorism and Effective Death Penalty Act of 1996 (AEDPA) prohibits federal courts from granting habeas relief unless the state court's decision "involved an unreasonable application of . . . *clearly established* Federal law, as determined by the Supreme Court of the United States." *28 U. S. C. § 2254(d)(1)* (emphasis added). As the dissenting judge below pointed out, no case of ours establishes, clearly or otherwise, that the *Confrontation Clause* bestows a right to *admit* this kind of evidence. *780 F. 3d, at 363-364* (opinion of Kethledge, J.). In fact we long ago suggested just the opposite. *Mattox v. United States, 156 U. S. 237, 245-250, 15 S. Ct. 337, 39 L. Ed. 409 (1895).* Each of the cases the Sixth Circuit relied on involved the defendant's attempting during cross-examination to impeach *testifying witnesses,* not unavailable declarants. See *Olden v. Kentucky, 488 U. S. 227, 230, 109 S. Ct. 480, 102 L. Ed. 2d 513 (1988) (per curiam); Delaware v. Van Arsdall, 475 U. S. 673, 676, 106 S. Ct. 1431, 89 L. Ed. 2d 674 (1986); Alford v. United States, 282 U. S. 687, 693, 51 S. Ct. 218, 75 L. Ed. 624 (1931).* And just recently we said in *Nevada v. Jackson, 569 U. S. ___, ___, 133 S. Ct. 1990, 186 L. Ed. 2d 62, 68 (2013) (per curiam),* that "this Court has never held that the *Confrontation Clause* entitles a criminal defendant to introduce *extrinsic evidence* for impeachment purposes." The Sixth Circuit thought the recantations here intrinsic, not extrinsic, and so beyond *Jackson*'s ambit. That is quite irrelevant. The pertinent question under AEDPA is whether our cases have clearly established a right, not whether they have failed to clearly foreclose it.

There may well be a plausible argument why the recantations ought to have been admitted under state law. See *Mich. Rule Evid. 806.* But nothing in our precedents clearly establishes their admissibility as a matter of federal constitutional law. AEDPA "provides a remedy for instances in which a state court unreasonably *applies* this Court's precedent; it does not require state courts to *extend* that precedent or license federal courts to treat the failure to do so as error." *White v. Woodall, 572 U. S. ___, ___, 134 S. Ct. 1697, 188 L. Ed. 2d 698, 702 (2014).* By framing the confrontation right at a high level of generality (making it the right "to impeach the credibility of an adverse witness"), the Sixth Circuit in effect "transform[ed] . . . [an] imaginative extension of existing case law into 'clearly established'" law. *Jackson, supra, at ___, 133 S. Ct. 1990, 186 L. Ed. 2d 62, 68*). That will not do.

The Sixth Circuit seems to have acquired a taste for disregarding AEDPA. *E.g., Woods v. Donald,* 575 U. S. ___, 135 S. Ct. 1372, 191 L. Ed. 2d 464 (2015) (*per curiam*); *White* v. *Woodall, supra; Burt v. Titlow,* 571 U. S. ___, 134 S. Ct. 10, 187 L. Ed. 2d 348 (2013); *Metrish v. Lancaster,* 569 U. S. ___, 133 S. Ct. 1781, 185 L. Ed. 2d 988 (2013); *Howes v. Fields,* 565 U. S. ___, 132 S. Ct. 1181, 182 L. Ed. 2d 17 (2012). We should grant certiorari to discourage this appetite.

Shapiro v. McManus

Supreme Court of the United States
November 4, 2015, Argued
December 8, 2015, Decided
No. 14-990.
136 S. Ct. 450

STEPHEN M. SHAPIRO, ET AL.,
PETITIONERS
v.
DAVID J. MCMANUS, JR.,
CHAIRMAN,
MARYLAND STATE BOARD OF ELECTIONS, ET AL.

Michael B. Kimberly argued the cause for petitioners.
Steven M. Sullivan argued the cause for respondents.

Unanimous decision.

Reversed and remanded.

JUSTICE SCALIA delivered the opinion of a unanimous Court.

We consider under what circumstances, if any, a district judge is free to "determin[e] that three judges are not required" for an action "challenging the constitutionality of the apportionment of congressional districts." *28 U. S. C. §§2284(a), (b)(1)*.

I

A

Rare today, three-judge district courts were more common in the decades before 1976, when they were required for various adjudications, including the grant of an "interlocutory or permanent injunction restraining the enforcement, operation or execution of any State statute . . . upon the ground of the unconstitutionality of such statute." *28 U. S. C. §2281 (1970 ed.)*, repealed, *Pub. L. 94-381, §1, 90 Stat. 1119*. See Currie, The Three-Judge District Court in Constitutional Litigation, 32 U. Chi. L. Rev. 1, 3-12 (1964). Decisions of three-judge courts could, then as now, be appealed as of right directly to this Court. *28 U. S. C. §1253*.

In 1976, Congress substantially curtailed the circumstances under which a three-judge court is required. It was no longer required for the grant of an injunction against state statutes, see *Pub. L. 94-381, §1, 90 Stat. 1119* (repealing *28 U. S. C. §2281*), but was mandated for "an action . . . challenging the constitutionality of the apportionment of congressional districts or the apportionment of any statewide legislative body." *Id., §3*, now codified at *28 U. S. C. §2284(a)*.

Simultaneously, Congress amended the procedures governing three-judge district courts. The prior statute had provided: "The district judge to whom the application for injunction or other relief is presented shall constitute one member of [the three-judge] court. On the filing of the application, he shall immediately notify the chief judge of the circuit, who shall designate two other judges" to serve. *28 U. S. C. §2284(1) (1970 ed.)*. The amended statute provides: "Upon the filing of a request for three judges, the judge to whom the request is presented shall, *unless he determines that three judges are not required*, immediately notify the chief judge of the circuit, who shall designate two other judges" to serve. *28*

U. S. C. §2284(b)(1) (2012 ed.) (emphasis added). The dispute here concerns the scope of the italicized text.

B

In response to the 2010 Census, Maryland enacted a statute in October 2011 establishing — or, more pejoratively, gerrymandering — the districts for the State's eight congressional seats. Dissatisfied with the crazy-quilt results, see App. to Pet. for Cert. 23a, petitioners, a bipartisan group of citizens, filed suit *pro se* in Federal District Court. Their amended complaint alleges, *inter alia*, that Maryland's redistricting plan burdens their *First Amendment* right of political association. Petitioners also requested that a three-judge court be convened to hear the case.

The District Judge, however, thought the claim "not one for which relief can be granted." *Benisek v. Mack, 11 F. Supp. 3d 516, 526 (Md. 2014).* "[N]othing about the congressional districts at issue in this case affects in any proscribed way [petitioners'] ability to participate in the political debate in any of the Maryland congressional districts in which they might find themselves. They are free to join preexisting political committees, form new ones, or use whatever other means are at their disposal to influence the opinions of their congressional representatives." *Ibid.* (brackets, ellipsis, and internal quotation marks omitted).

For that reason, instead of notifying the Chief Judge of the Circuit of the need for a three-judge court, the District Judge dismissed the action. The Fourth Circuit summarily affirmed in an unpublished disposition. *Benisek v. Mack, 584 Fed. Appx. 140 (CA4 2014).* Seeking review in this Court, petitioners pointed out that at least two other Circuits consider it reversible error for a district judge to dismiss a case under §2284 for failure to state a claim for relief rather than refer it for transfer to a three-judge court. See *LaRouche v. Fowler, 152 F. 3d 974, 981-983, 332 U.S. App. D.C. 25 (CADC 1998); LULAC v. Texas, 113 F. 3d 53, 55-56 (CA5 1997) (per curiam).* We granted certiorari. *Shapiro v. Mack, 576 U. S. ___, 135 S. Ct. 2805, 192 L. Ed. 2d 846 (2015).*

II

Petitioners' sole contention is that the District Judge had no authority to dismiss the case rather than initiate the procedures to convene a three-judge court. Not so, argue respondents; the 1976 addition to *§2284(b)(1)* of the clause "unless he determines that three judges are not required" is precisely such a grant of authority. Moreover, say respondents, Congress declined to specify a standard to constrain the exercise of this authority. Choosing, as the District Judge did, the familiar standard for dismissal under *Federal Rule of Civil Procedure 12(b)(6)* best serves the purposes of a three-judge court, which (in respondents' view) is to protect States from "hasty, imprudent invalidation" of their statutes by rogue district judges acting alone. Brief for Respondents 27.

Whatever the purposes of a three-judge court may be, respondents' argument needlessly produces a contradiction in the statutory text. That text's initial prescription could not be clearer: "A district court of three judges *shall be convened* . . . when an action is filed challenging the constitutionality of the apportionment of congressional districts . . . ." *28 U. S. C. §2284(a)* (emphasis added). Nobody disputes that the present suit is "an action . . . challenging the constitutionality of the apportionment of congressional districts." It follows that the district judge was *required* to refer the case to a three-judge court, for *§2284(a)* admits of no exception, and "the mandatory 'shall'. . . normally creates an obligation impervious to judicial discretion." *Lexecon Inc. v. Milberg Weiss Bershad Hynes & Lerach, 523 U. S. 26, 35, 118 S. Ct. 956, 140 L. Ed. 2d 62 (1998)*; see also *National Assn. of Home Builders v. Defenders of Wildlife, 551 U. S. 644, 661-662, 127 S. Ct. 2518, 168 L. Ed. 2d 467 (2007)* (same).

The subsequent provision of *§2284(b)(1)*, that the district judge shall commence the process for appointment of a three-judge panel "unless he determines that three judges are not required," need not and therefore should not be read as a grant of discretion to the district judge to ignore *§2284(a)*. It is not even framed as a proviso, or an exception from that provision, but rather as an administrative detail that is entirely compatible with *§2284(a)*. The old *§2284(1)* triggered the district judge's duty to refer the matter for the convening of a three-judge court "[o]n the filing of the application" to enjoin an unconstitutional state law. By contrast, the current *§2284(b)(1)* triggers the district judge's duty "[u]pon the filing of a *request* for three judges" (emphasis added). But of course a party may — whether in good faith or bad, through ignorance or hope or malice — file a *request* for a three-judge court even if the case does not merit one under *§2284(a)*. *Section 2284(b)(1)* merely clarifies that a district judge need not unthinkingly initiate the procedures to convene a three-judge court without first examining the allegations in the complaint. In short, all the district judge must "determin[e]" is whether the "request for three judges" is made in a case covered by *§2284(a)* — no more, no less.

That conclusion is bolstered by *§2284(b)(3)*'s explicit command that "[a] single judge shall not . . . enter judgment on the merits." It would be an odd interpretation that allowed a district judge to do under *§2284(b)(1)* what he is forbidden to do under *§2284(b)(3)*. More likely that Congress intended a three-judge court, and not a single district judge, to enter all final judgments in cases satisfying the criteria of *§2284(a)*.

III

Respondents argue in the alternative that a district judge is not required to refer a case for the convening of a three-judge court if the constitutional claim is (as they assert petitioners' claim to be) "insubstantial." In *Goosby v. Osser, 409 U. S. 512, 93 S. Ct. 854, 35 L. Ed. 2d 36 (1973)*, we stated that the filing of a "constitutionally insubstantial" claim did not trigger the three-judge-court requirement under the pre-1976 statutory regime. *Id., at 518, 93 S. Ct. 854, 35 L. Ed. 2d 36*. *Goosby* rested not on an interpretation of statutory text, but on the familiar proposition that "[i]n the absence of diversity of citizenship, it is essential to jurisdiction that a *substantial* federal question should be presented." *Ex parte Poresky, 290 U. S. 30, 31, 54 S. Ct. 3, 78 L. Ed. 152 (1933) (per curiam)* (emphasis added). Absent a substantial federal question, even a single-judge district court lacks jurisdiction, and "[a] three-judge court is not required where the district court itself lacks jurisdiction of the complaint or the complaint is not justiciable in the federal courts." *Gonzalez v. Automatic Employees Credit Union, 419 U. S. 90, 100, 95 S. Ct. 289, 42 L. Ed. 2d 249 (1974)*.

In the present case, however, the District Judge dismissed petitioners' complaint not because he thought he lacked jurisdiction, but because he concluded that the allegations failed to state a claim for relief on the merits, citing *Ashcroft v. Iqbal, 556 U. S. 662, 129 S. Ct. 1937, 173 L. Ed. 2d 868 (2009)*, and *Bell Atlantic Corp. v. Twombly, 550 U. S. 544, 127 S. Ct. 1955, 167 L. Ed. 2d 929 (2007)*. See *11 F. Supp. 3d, at 520*. That was in accord with Fourth Circuit precedent, which holds that where the "pleadings do not state a claim, then *by definition they are insubstantial* and so properly are subject to dismissal by the district court without convening a three-judge court." *Duckworth v. State Admin. Bd. of Election Laws, 332 F. 3d 769, 772-773 (CA4 2003)* (emphasis added).

We think this standard both too demanding and inconsistent with our precedents. "[C]onstitutional claims will not lightly be found insubstantial for purposes of" the three-judge-court statute. *Washington v. Confederated Tribes of Colville Reservation, 447 U. S. 134, 147-148, 100 S. Ct. 2069, 65 L. Ed. 2d 10 (1980)*. We have long distinguished between failing to raise a substantial federal question for jurisdictional purposes—which is what *Goosby* addressed—and failing to state a claim for relief on the merits; only "wholly insubstantial and frivolous" claims implicate the former. *Bell v. Hood, 327 U. S. 678, 682-683, 66 S. Ct. 773, 90 L. Ed. 939 (1946)*; see also *Hannis Distilling Co. v. Mayor and City Council of Baltimore, 216 U. S. 285, 288, 30 S. Ct. 326, 54 L. Ed. 482 (1910)* ("obviously frivolous or plainly insubstantial"); *Bailey v. Patterson, 369 U. S. 31, 33, 82 S. Ct. 549, 7 L. Ed. 2d 512 (1962)* (*per curiam*) ("wholly insubstantial," "legally speaking non-existent," "essentially fictitious"); *Steel Co. v. Citizens for Better Environment, 523 U. S. 83, 89, 118 S. Ct. 1003, 140 L. Ed. 2d 210 (1998)* ("frivolous or immaterial"). Absent such frivolity, "the failure to state a proper cause of action calls for a judgment on the merits and not for a dismissal for want of jurisdiction." *Bell, supra, at 682, 66 S. Ct. 773, 90 L. Ed. 939*. Consistent with this principle, *Goosby* clarified that "'[c]onstitutional insubstantiality' for this purpose has been equated with such concepts as 'essentially fictitious,' 'wholly insubstantial,' 'obviously frivolous,' and 'obviously without merit.'" *409 U. S., at 518, 93 S. Ct. 854, 35 L. Ed. 2d 36* (citations omitted). And the adverbs were no mere throwaways; "[t]he limiting words 'wholly' and 'obviously' have cogent legal significance." *Ibid.*

Without expressing any view on the merits of petitioners' claim, we believe it easily clears *Goosby's* low bar; after all, the amended complaint specifically challenges Maryland's apportionment "along the lines

23

suggested by Justice Kennedy in his concurrence in *Vieth [v. Jubelirer, 541 U. S. 267, 124 S. Ct. 1769, 158 L. Ed. 2d 546 (2004)]*." App. to Brief in Opposition 44. Although the *Vieth* plurality thought all political gerrymandering claims nonjusticiable, JUSTICE KENNEDY, concurring in the judgment, surmised that if "a State did impose burdens and restrictions on groups or persons by reason of their views, there would likely be a *First Amendment* violation, unless the State shows some compelling interest. . . . Where it is alleged that a gerrymander had the purpose and effect of imposing burdens on a disfavored party and its voters, the *First Amendment* may offer a sounder and more prudential basis for intervention than does the *Equal Protection Clause*." *Vieth v. Jubelirer, 541 U. S. 267, 315, 124 S. Ct. 1769, 158 L. Ed. 2d 546 (2004)*. Whatever "wholly insubstantial," "obviously frivolous," etc., mean, at a minimum they cannot include a plea for relief based on a legal theory put forward by a Justice of this Court and uncontradicted by the majority in any of our cases. Accordingly, the District Judge should not have dismissed the claim as "constitutionally insubstantial" under *Goosby*. Perhaps petitioners will ultimately fail on the merits of their suit, but *§2284* entitles them to make their case before a three-judge district court.

***

The judgment of the Fourth Circuit is reversed, and the case is remanded for further proceedings consistent with this opinion.

It is so ordered.

Kansas v. Carr

Supreme Court of the United States
October 7, 2015, Argued
January 20, 2016, Decided
Nos. 14-449, 14-450, and 14-452.
136 S. Ct. 633

KANSAS, PETITIONER	KANSAS, PETITIONER	KANSAS, PETITIONER
v.	v.	v.
JONATHAN D. CARR	REGINALD DEXTER CARR, JR.	SIDNEY J. GLEASON

Derek L. Schmidt argued the cause for petitioner on the burden question.

Stephen R. McAllister argued the cause for petitioner on the severance question.

Rachel P. Kovner argued the cause for the United States, as amicus curiae, by special leave of court, on the severance question.

Jeffrey T. Green argued the cause for respondents in No. 14-449 and No. 14-452 on the burden question.

Neal K. Katyal argued the cause for respondent in No. 14-450 on the burden question.

Frederick Liu argued the cause for respondent in No. 14-450 on the severance question.

Jeffrey T. Green argued the cause for respondent in No. 14-449 on the severance question.

SCALIA, J., delivered the opinion of the Court, in which ROBERTS, C. J., and KENNEDY, THOMAS, GINSBURG, BREYER, ALITO, and KAGAN, JJ., joined. SOTOMAYOR, J., filed a dissenting opinion.

8-1 Decision; 1 Dissent.

Reversed and remanded.

JUSTICE SCALIA delivered the opinion of the Court.

The Supreme Court of Kansas vacated the death sentences of Sidney Gleason and brothers Reginald and Jonathan Carr. Gleason killed one of his co-conspirators and her boyfriend to cover up the robbery of an elderly man. The Carrs' notorious Wichita crime spree culminated in the brutal rape, robbery, kidnaping, and execution-style shooting of five young men and women. We first consider whether the Constitution required the sentencing courts to instruct the juries that mitigating circumstances "need not be proved beyond a reasonable doubt." And second, whether the Constitution required severance of the Carrs' joint sentencing proceedings.

I

A

Less than one month after Sidney Gleason was paroled from his sentence for attempted voluntary manslaughter, he joined a conspiracy to rob an elderly man at knifepoint. [1] Gleason and a companion "cut up" the elderly man to get $10 to $35 and a box of cigarettes. *299 Kan. 1127, 1136, 329 P. 3d 1102, 1115 (2014)*. Fearing that their female co-conspirators would snitch, Gleason and his cousin, Damien Thompson, set out to kill co-conspirator Mikiala Martinez. Gleason shot and killed Martinez's boyfriend, and then Gleason and Thompson drove Martinez to a rural location, where Thompson strangled her for five minutes and then shot her in the chest, Gleason standing by and providing the gun for the final shot.

The State ultimately charged Gleason with capital murder for killing Martinez and her boyfriend, first-degree premeditated murder of the boyfriend, aggravating kidnaping of Martinez, attempted first-degree murder and aggravated robbery of the elderly man, and criminal possession of a firearm. He was convicted on all counts except the attempted first-degree murder charge. *Id., at 1134-1135, 1146, 329 P. 3d, at 1114, 1120*. The jury also found that the State proved beyond a reasonable doubt the existence of four aggravating circumstances and

---

[1] The facts for this portion of the opinion come from the Kansas Supreme Court, *299 Kan. 1127, 1134-1147, 329 P. 3d 1102, 1113-1121 (2014)*, and the parties' briefs.

unanimously agreed to a sentence of death. *Id., at 1146-1147, 329 P. 3d, at 1120-1121.*

B

In December 2000, brothers Reginald and Jonathan Carr set out on a crime spree culminating in the Wichita Massacre. [2] On the night of December 7, Reginald Carr and an unknown man carjacked Andrew Schreiber, held a gun to his head, and forced him to make cash withdrawals at various ATMs.

On the night of December 11, the brothers followed Linda Ann Walenta, a cellist for the Wichita symphony, home from orchestra practice. One of them approached her vehicle and said he needed help. When she rolled down her window, he pointed a gun at her head. When she shifted into reverse to escape, he shot her three times, ran back to his brother's car, and fled the scene. One of the gunshots severed Walenta's spine, and she died one month later as a result of her injuries.

On the night of December 14, the brothers burst into a triplex at 12727 Birchwood, where roommates Jason, Brad, and Aaron lived. Jason's girlfriend, Holly, and Heather, a friend of Aaron's, were also in the house. Armed with handguns and a golf club, the brothers forced all five into Jason's bedroom. They demanded that they strip naked and later ordered them into the bedroom closet. They took Holly and Heather from the bedroom, demanded that they perform oral sex and digitally penetrate each other as the Carrs looked on and barked orders. They forced each of the men to have sex with Holly and then with Heather. They yelled that the men would be shot if they could not have sex with the women, so Holly—fearing for Jason's life—performed oral sex on him in the closet before he was ordered out by the brothers.

---

[2] The facts for this portion of the opinion come from the Kansas Supreme Court, *300 Kan. 1, 18-38, 331 P. 3d 544, 575-586 (2014)*, and witness testimony. See 21-A Tr. 59-75 (Oct. 7, 2002), 22-B Tr. 39-124 (Oct. 8, 2002), 23-A Tr. 4-118 (Oct. 9, 2002), 23-B Tr. 5-133 (Oct. 9, 2002), and 24-A Tr. 4-93 (Oct. 10, 2002).

Jonathan then snatched Holly from the closet. He ordered that she digitally penetrate herself. He set his gun between her knees on the floor. And he raped her. Then he raped Heather.

Reginald took Brad, Jason, Holly, and Aaron one-by-one to various ATMs to withdraw cash. When the victims returned to the house, their torture continued. Holly urinated in the closet because of fright. Jonathan found an engagement ring hidden in the bedroom that Jason was keeping as a surprise for Holly. Pointing his gun at Jason, he had Jason identify the ring while Holly was sitting nearby in the closet. Then Reginald took Holly from the closet, said he was not going to shoot her yet, and raped her on the dining-room floor strewn with boxes of Christmas decorations. He forced her to turn around, ejaculated into her mouth, and forced her to swallow. In a nearby bathroom, Jonathan again raped Heather and then again raped Holly.

At 2 a.m.—three hours after the mayhem began—the brothers decided it was time to leave the house. They attempted to put all five victims in the trunk of Aaron's Honda Civic. Finding that they would not all fit, they jammed the three young men into the trunk. They directed Heather to the front of the car and Holly to Jason's pickup truck, driven by Reginald. Once the vehicles arrived at a snow-covered field, they instructed Jason and Brad, still naked, and Aaron to kneel in the snow. Holly cried, "Oh, my God, they're going to shoot us." Holly and Heather were then ordered to kneel in the snow. Holly went to Jason's side; Heather, to Aaron.

Holly heard the first shot, heard Aaron plead with the brothers not to shoot, heard the second shot, heard the screams, heard the third shot, and the fourth. She felt the blow of the fifth shot to her head, but remained kneeling. They kicked her so she would fall face-first into the snow and ran her over in the pickup truck. But she survived, because a hair clip she had fastened to her hair that night deflected the bullet. She went to Jason, took off her sweater, the only scrap of clothing the brothers had let her wear, and tied it around his head to stop the bleeding from his eye. She rushed to Brad, then Aaron, and then Heather.

Spotting a house with white Christmas lights in the distance, Holly started running toward it for help—naked, skull shattered, and without shoes, through the snow and over barbed-wire fences. Each time a car passed on the nearby road, she feared it was the brothers returning and camouflaged herself by lying down in the snow. She made it to the house, rang the doorbell, knocked. A man opened the door, and she relayed as quickly as she could the events of the night to him, and minutes later to a 911 dispatcher, fearing that she would not live.

Holly lived, and retold this play-by-play of the night's events to the jury. Investigators also testified that the brothers returned to the Birchwood house after leaving the five friends for dead, where they ransacked the place for valuables and (for good measure) beat Holly's dog, Nikki, to death with a golf club.

The State charged each of the brothers with more than 50 counts, including murder, rape, sodomy, kidnaping, burglary, and robbery, and the jury returned separate guilty verdicts. It convicted Reginald of one count of kidnaping, aggravated robbery, aggravated battery, and criminal damage to property for the Schreiber carjacking, and one count of first-degree felony murder for the Walenta shooting. Jonathan was acquitted of all counts related to the Schreiber carjacking but convicted of first-degree felony murder for the Walenta shooting. For the Birchwood murders, the jury convicted each brother of 4 counts of capital murder, 1 count of attempted first-degree murder, 5 counts of aggravated kidnaping, 9 counts of aggravated robbery, 20 counts of rape or attempted rape, 3 counts of aggravated criminal sodomy, 1 count each of aggravated burglary and burglary, 1 count of theft, and 1 count of cruelty to animals. The jury also convicted Reginald of three counts of unlawful possession of a firearm. *300 Kan. 1, 15-16, 331 P. 3d 544, 573-574 (2014)*.

The State sought the death penalty for each of the four Birchwood murders, and the brothers were sentenced together. The State relied on the guilt-phase evidence, including Holly's two days of testimony, as evidence of four aggravating circumstances: that the defendants knowingly or purposely killed or created a great risk of death to more than one person; that they committed the crimes for the purpose of receiving money or items of monetary value; that they committed the crimes to prevent arrest or prosecution; and that they committed the crimes in an especially heinous, atrocious, or cruel manner. *Id., at 258-259, 331 P. 3d, at 708*. After hearing each brother's case for mitigation, the jury issued separate verdicts of death for Reginald and Jonathan. It found unanimously that the State proved the existence of the four aggravating circumstances beyond a reasonable doubt and that those aggravating circumstances outweighed the mitigating circumstances, justifying four separate verdicts of death for each brother for the murders of Jason, Brad, Aaron, and Heather. App. in No. 14-449 etc., pp. 461-492.

C

The Kansas Supreme Court vacated the death penalties in both cases. It held that the instructions used in both Gleason's and the Carrs' sentencing violated the *Eighth Amendment* because they "failed to affirmatively inform the jury that mitigating circumstances need only be proved to the satisfaction of the individual juror in that juror's sentencing decision and not beyond a reasonable doubt." *299 Kan., at 1196, 329 P. 3d, at 1147* (Gleason); *300 Kan., at 303, 331 P. 3d, at 733* (Reginald Carr); *300 Kan. 340, 369-370, 329 P. 3d 1195, 1213* (2014) (Jonathan Carr). Without that instruction, according to the court, the jury "was left to speculate as to the correct burden of proof for mitigating circumstances, and reasonable jurors might have believed they could not consider mitigating circumstances not proven beyond a reasonable doubt." *299 Kan., at 1197, 329 P. 3d, at 1148.* This, the court concluded, might have caused jurors to exclude relevant mitigating evidence from their consideration. *Ibid.*

The Kansas Supreme Court also held that the Carrs' death sentences had to be vacated because of the trial court's failure to sever their sentencing proceedings, thereby violating the brothers' *Eighth Amendment* right "to an individualized capital sentencing determination." *300 Kan., at 275, 331 P. 3d, at 717; 300 Kan., at 368, 329 P. 3d, at 1212.* According to the court, the joint trial "inhibited the jury's individualized consideration of [Jonathan] because of family characteristics tending to demonstrate future dangerousness that he shared with his brother"; and his brother's visible handcuffs prejudiced the jury's consideration of his sentence. *300 Kan., at 275, 331 P. 3d, at 717.* As for Reginald, he was prejudiced, according to the Kansas Supreme Court, by Jonathan's portrayal of him as the corrupting older brother. *Id., at 276, 331 P. 3d, at 717.* Moreover, Reginald was prejudiced by his brother's cross-examination of their sister, who testified that she thought Reginald had admitted to her that he was the shooter. *Id., at 279, 331 P. 3d, at 719.* (She later backtracked and testified, "'I don't remember who was, you know, shot by who[m].'" *Ibid.*) The Kansas Supreme Court opined that the presumption that the jury followed its instructions to consider each defendant separately was "defeated by logic." *Id., at 280, 331 P. 3d, at 719.* "[T]he defendants' joint upbringing in the maelstrom that was their family and their influence on and interactions with one another . . . simply was not amenable to orderly separation and analysis." *Ibid., 331 P. 3d, at 719-720.* The Kansas Supreme Court found itself unable to "say that the death verdict was unattributable, at least in part, to this error." *Id., at 282, 331 P. 3d, at 720.* We granted certiorari. *575 U. S. ___, 135 S. Ct. 1698, 191 L. Ed. 2d 674 (2015).*

II

We first turn to the Kansas Supreme Court's contention that the *Eighth Amendment* required these capital-sentencing courts to instruct the jury that mitigating circumstances need not be proved beyond a reasonable doubt.

A

Before considering the merits of that contention, we consider Gleason's challenge to our jurisdiction. According to Gleason, the Kansas Supreme Court's decision rests on adequate and independent state-law grounds. This argument is a familiar one. We rejected it in *Kansas v. Marsh, 548 U. S. 163, 169, 126 S. Ct. 2516, 165 L. Ed. 2d 429 (2006).* Like the defendant in that case, Gleason urges that the decision below rests only on a rule of Kansas law announced in *State v. Kleypas, 272 Kan. 894, 40 P. 3d 139 (2001) (per curiam)*—a rule later reiterated in *State v. Scott, 286 Kan. 54, 183 P. 3d 801 (2008) (per curiam).* As we stated in *Marsh, "Kleypas,* itself, rested on federal law." *548 U. S., at 169, 126 S. Ct. 2516, 165 L. Ed. 2d 429.* So too does the relevant passage of *Scott,* which rested on *Kleypas*'s discussion of the constitutional rule that jurors need not agree on mitigating circumstances. See *Scott, supra, at 106-107, 183 P. 3d, at 837-838.* The Kansas Supreme Court's opinion in this case acknowledged as much, saying that "statements from *Kleypas* implicate the broader *Eighth Amendment* principle prohibiting barriers that preclude a sentencer's consideration of all relevant mitigating evidence." *299 Kan., at 1195, 329 P. 3d, at 1147.*

The Kansas Supreme Court's opinion leaves no room for doubt that it was relying on the Federal Constitution. It stated that the instruction it required "protects a capital defendant's *Eighth Amendment* right to individualized sentencing," that the absence of the instruction "implicat[ed] Gleason's right to individualized sentencing under the *Eighth Amendment,*" and that vacatur of Gleason's death sentence was the "[c]onsequen[ce]" of *Eighth Amendment* error. *Id., at 1196-1197, 329 P. 3d, at 1147-1148* (emphasis added).

For this reason, the criticism leveled by the dissent is misdirected. It generally would have been "none of our business" had the Kansas Supreme Court vacated Gleason's and the Carrs' death sentences on state-law grounds. *Marsh, 548 U. S., at 184, 126 S. Ct. 2516, 165 L. Ed. 2d 429* (SCALIA, J., concurring). But it decidedly did not. And when the Kansas Supreme Court time and again invalidates death sentences because it says the Federal Constitution *requires* it, "review by this Court, far from *undermining* state autonomy, is the only possible way to *vindicate* it." *Ibid.* "When we correct a state court's federal errors, *we return power to the State, and to its people.*" *Ibid.* The state courts may experiment all they want with their own constitutions, and often do in the wake of this Court's decisions. See Sutton, *San Antonio Independent School District v. Rodriguez* And Its Aftermath, *94 Va. L. Rev. 1963, 1971-1977 (2008).* But what a state court cannot do is experiment with our Federal Constitution and expect to elude this Court's review so long as victory goes to the criminal defendant. "Turning a blind eye" in such cases "would change the uniform 'law of the land' into a crazy quilt." *Marsh, supra, at 185, 126 S. Ct. 2516, 165 L. Ed. 2d 429.* And it would enable state courts to blame the unpopular death-sentence reprieve of the most horrible criminals upon the Federal Constitution when it is in fact their own doing.

B

We turn, then, to the merits of the Kansas Supreme Court's conclusion that the *Eighth Amendment* requires capital-sentencing courts in Kansas "to affirmatively inform the jury that mitigating circumstances need not be proven beyond a reasonable doubt." *299 Kan., at 1197, 329 P. 3d, at 1148.*

Approaching the question in the abstract, and without reference to our capital-sentencing case law, we doubt whether it is even possible to apply a standard of proof to the mitigating-factor determination (the so-called "selection phase" of a capital-sentencing proceeding). It is possible to do so for the aggravating-factor determination (the so-called "eligibility phase"), because that is a purely factual determination. The facts justifying death set forth in the Kansas statute either did or did not exist—and one can require the finding that they did exist to be made beyond a reasonable doubt. Whether mitigation exists, however, is largely a judgment call (or perhaps a value call); what one juror might consider mitigating another might not. And of course the ultimate question whether mitigating circumstances outweigh aggravating circumstances is mostly a question of mercy—the quality of which, as we know, is not strained. It would mean nothing, we think, to tell the jury that the defendants must deserve mercy beyond a reasonable doubt; or must more-likely-than-not deserve it. It *would* be possible, of course, to instruct the jury that *the facts establishing* mitigating circumstances need only be proved by a preponderance, leaving the judgment whether those facts are indeed mitigating, and whether they outweigh the aggravators, to the jury's discretion without a standard of proof. If we were to hold that the Constitution requires the mitigating-factor determination to be divided into its factual component and its judgmental component, and the former to be accorded a burden-of-proof instruction, we doubt whether that would produce anything but jury confusion. In the last analysis, jurors will accord mercy if they deem it appropriate, and withhold mercy if they do not, which is what our case law is designed to achieve.

In any event, our case law does not require capital sentencing courts "to affirmatively inform the jury that mitigating circumstances need not be proved beyond a reasonable doubt." *Ibid.* In *Buchanan v. Angelone, 522 U. S. 269, 118 S. Ct. 757, 139 L. Ed. 2d 702 (1998),* we upheld a death sentence even though the trial court "failed to provide the jury with express guidance on the concept of mitigation." *Id., at 275, 118 S. Ct. 757, 139 L. Ed. 2d 702.* Likewise in *Weeks v. Angelone, 528 U. S. 225, 120 S. Ct. 727, 145 L. Ed. 2d 727 (2000),* we reaffirmed that the Court has "never held that the State must structure in a particular way the manner in which juries consider mitigating evidence" and rejected the contention that it was constitutionally deficient to instruct jurors to "'consider a mitigating circumstance if you find there is evidence to support it,'" without additional guidance. *Id., at 232-233, 120 S. Ct. 727, 145 L. Ed. 2d 727.*

Equally unavailing is the contention that even if an instruction that mitigating evidence need not be "proven beyond a reasonable doubt" is not always required, it was constitutionally necessary in *these* cases to avoid confusion. Ambiguity in capital-sentencing instructions gives rise to constitutional error only if "there is a *reasonable likelihood* that the jury has applied the challenged instruction in a way that prevents the consideration of constitutionally relevant evidence." *Boyde v. California, 494 U. S. 370, 380, 110 S. Ct. 1190, 108 L. Ed. 2d 316 (1990)* (emphasis added). The alleged confusion stemming from the jury instructions used at the defendants' sentencings does not clear that bar. A meager "possibility" of confusion is not enough. *Ibid.*

As an initial matter, the defendants' argument rests on the assumption that it would be unconstitutional to require the defense to prove mitigating circumstances beyond a reasonable doubt. Assuming without deciding that that is the case, the record belies the defendants' contention that the instructions caused jurors to apply that standard of proof. The defendants focus upon the following instruction: "The State has the burden to prove beyond a reasonable doubt that there are one or more aggravating circumstances and that they are not outweighed by any mitigating circumstances found to exist." App. to Pet. for Cert. in No. 14-452, p. 133 (Instr. 8). [3] The juxtaposition of aggravating and mitigating circumstances, so goes the argument, caused the jury to speculate that mitigating circumstances must also be proved beyond a reasonable doubt. *299 Kan., at 1197, 329 P. 3d, at 1148.* It seems to us quite the opposite. The instruction makes clear that both the existence of aggravating circumstances and the conclusion that they outweigh mitigating circumstances must be proved beyond a reasonable doubt; mitigating circumstances themselves, on the other hand, must merely be "found to exist." That same description, mitigating circumstances *"found to exist,"* is contained in three other instructions, App. to Pet. for

---

[3] The relevant penalty-phase instructions from the Carrs' sentencing proceedings are materially indistinguishable. See App. to Pet. for Cert. in No. 14-450, pp. 501-510.

Cert. in No. 14-452, at 133 (Instrs. 7, 9, and 10) (emphasis added)—unsurprisingly, since it recites the Kansas statute, see *Kan. Stat. Ann. §21-4624(e)* (1995). "Found to exist" certainly does not suggest proof beyond a reasonable doubt. The instructions as a whole distinguish clearly between aggravating and mitigating circumstances: "*The State* has the burden to prove beyond a reasonable doubt that there are one or more aggravating circumstances . . .," and the jury must decide unanimously that the State met that burden. App. to Pet. for Cert. in No. 14-452, at 133 (Instrs. 8 and 10) (emphasis added). "Mitigating circumstances," on the other hand, "do not need to be found by all members of the jury" to "be considered by an individual juror in arriving at his or her sentencing decision." *Id.*, at 131 (Instr. 7). Not once do the instructions say that defense counsel bears the burden of proving the facts constituting a mitigating circumstance beyond a reasonable doubt—nor would that make much sense, since one of the mitigating circumstances is (curiously) "mercy," which simply is not a factual determination.

We reject the Kansas Supreme Court's decision that jurors were "left to speculate as to the correct burden of proof for mitigating circumstances." *299 Kan., at 1197, 329 P. 3d, at 1148.* For the reasons we have described, no juror would reasonably have speculated that mitigating circumstances must be proved by any particular standard, let alone beyond a reasonable doubt. The reality is that jurors do not "pars[e] instructions for subtle shades of meaning in the same way that lawyers might." *Boyde, supra, at 381, 110 S. Ct. 1190, 108 L. Ed. 2d 316.* The instructions repeatedly told the jurors to consider *any* mitigating factor, meaning any aspect of the defendants' background or the circumstances of their offense. Jurors would not have misunderstood these instructions to prevent their consideration of constitutionally relevant evidence.

III

We turn next to the contention that a joint capital-sentencing proceeding in the Carrs' cases violated the defendants' *Eighth Amendment* right to an "individualized sentencing determination." *300 Kan., at 276, 331 P. 3d, at 717.*

The Kansas Supreme Court agreed with the defendants that, because of the joint sentencing proceeding, one defendant's mitigating evidence put a thumb on death's scale for the other, in violation of the other's *Eighth Amendment* rights. *Ibid.* It accepted Reginald's contention that he was prejudiced by his brother's portrayal of him as the corrupting older brother. And it agreed that Reginald was prejudiced by his brother's cross-examination of their sister, who equivocated about whether Reginald admitted to her that he was the shooter. (Reginald has all but abandoned that implausible theory of prejudice before this Court and contends only that the State "likely would not have introduced any such testimony" had he been sentenced alone. Brief for Respondent in No. 14-450, p. 34, n. 3.) Jonathan asserted that he was prejudiced by evidence associating him with his dangerous older brother, which caused the jury to perceive him as an incurable sociopath. [4] Both speculate that the evidence assertedly prejudicial to them would have been inadmissible in severed proceedings under Kansas law. The Kansas Supreme Court also launched a broader attack on the joint proceedings, contending that the joinder rendered it impossible for the jury to consider the Carrs' relative moral culpability and to determine individually whether they were entitled to "mercy." *300 Kan., at 278, 331 P. 3d, at 718-719.*

Whatever the merits of defendants' procedural objections, we will not shoehorn them into the *Eighth Amendment*'s prohibition of "cruel and unusual punishments." As the United States as *amicus curiae* intimates, the *Eighth Amendment* is inapposite when each defendant's claim is, at bottom, that the jury considered evidence that would not have been admitted in a severed proceeding, and that the joint trial clouded the jury's consideration of mitigating evidence like "mercy." Brief for United States 24, n. 8. As we held in *Romano v. Oklahoma, 512 U. S. 1, 114 S. Ct. 2004, 129 L. Ed. 2d 1 (1994)*, it is not the role of the *Eighth Amendment* to establish a special "federal code of evidence" governing "the admissibility of evidence at capital sentencing proceedings." *Id., at 11-12, 114 S. Ct. 2004, 129 L. Ed. 2d 1.* Rather, it is the *Due Process Clause* that wards off the introduction of "unduly prejudicial" evidence

---

[4] Jonathan also alleges that he was prejudiced by the jury's witnessing his brother's handcuffs, which his brother requested remain visible before the penalty phase commenced. That allegation is mystifying. That his brother's handcuffs were visible (while his own restraints were not) more likely caused the jury to see Jonathan as the *less* dangerous of the two.

that would "rende[r] the trial fundamentally unfair." *Payne v. Tennessee, 501 U. S. 808, 825, 111 S. Ct. 2597, 115 L. Ed. 2d 720 (1991)*; see also *Brown v. Sanders, 546 U. S. 212, 220-221, 126 S. Ct. 884, 163 L. Ed. 2d 723 (2006)*.

The test prescribed by *Romano* for a constitutional violation attributable to evidence improperly admitted at a capital-sentencing proceeding is whether the evidence "so infected the sentencing proceeding with unfairness as to render the jury's imposition of the death penalty a denial of due process." *512 U. S., at 12, 114 S. Ct. 2004, 129 L. Ed. 2d 1*. The mere admission of evidence that might not otherwise have been admitted in a severed proceeding does not demand the automatic vacatur of a death sentence.

In light of all the evidence presented at the guilt and penalty phases relevant to the jury's sentencing determination, the contention that the admission of mitigating evidence by one brother could have "so infected" the jury's consideration of the other's sentence as to amount to a denial of due process is beyond the pale. To begin with, the court instructed the jury that it "must give separate consideration to each defendant," that each was "entitled to have his sentence decided on the evidence and law which is applicable to him," and that any evidence in the penalty phase "limited to only one defendant should not be considered by you as to the other defendant." App. to Pet. for Cert. in No. 14-450, at 501 (Instr. 3). The court gave defendant-specific instructions for aggravating and mitigating circumstances. *Id.*, at 502-508 (Instrs. 5, 6, 7, and 8). And the court instructed the jury to consider the "individual" or "particular defendant" by using four separate verdict forms for each defendant, one for each murdered occupant of the Birchwood house. *Id.*, at 509 (Instr. 10); App. in No. 14-449 etc., at 461-492. We presume the jury followed these instructions and considered each defendant separately when deciding to impose a sentence of death for each of the brutal murders. *Romano, supra, at 13, 114 S. Ct. 2004, 129 L. Ed. 2d 1*.

The contrary conclusion of the Kansas Supreme Court—that the presumption that jurors followed these instructions was "defeated by logic," *300 Kan., at 280, 331 P. 3d, at 719*—is untenable. The Carrs implausibly liken the prejudice resulting from the joint sentencing proceeding to the prejudice infecting the joint trial in *Bruton v. United States, 391 U. S. 123, 88 S. Ct. 1620, 20 L. Ed. 2d 476 (1968)*, where the prosecution admitted hearsay evidence of a codefendant's confession implicating the defendant. That particular violation of the defendant's confrontation rights, incriminating evidence of the most persuasive sort, ineradicable, as a practical matter, from the jury's mind, justified what we have described as a narrow departure from the presumption that jurors follow their instructions, *Richardson v. Marsh, 481 U. S. 200, 207, 107 S. Ct. 1702, 95 L. Ed. 2d 176 (1987).* We have declined to extend that exception, *id., at 211, 107 S. Ct. 1702, 95 L. Ed. 2d 176,* and have continued to apply the presumption to instructions regarding mitigating evidence in capital-sentencing proceedings, see, *e.g., Weeks, 528 U. S., at 234, 120 S. Ct. 727, 145 L. Ed. 2d 727.* There is no reason to think the jury could not follow its instruction to consider the defendants separately in this case.

Joint proceedings are not only permissible but are often preferable when the joined defendants' criminal conduct arises out of a single chain of events. Joint trial may enable a jury "to arrive more reliably at its conclusions regarding the guilt or innocence of a particular defendant and to assign fairly the respective responsibilities of each defendant in the sentencing." *Buchanan v. Kentucky, 483 U. S. 402, 418, 107 S. Ct. 2906, 97 L. Ed. 2d 336 (1987).* That the codefendants might have "antagonistic" theories of mitigation, *Zafiro v. United States, 506 U. S. 534, 538, 113 S. Ct. 933, 122 L. Ed. 2d 317 (1993),* does not suffice to overcome Kansas's "interest in promoting the reliability and consistency of its judicial process," *Buchanan, supra, at 418, 107 S. Ct. 2906, 97 L. Ed. 2d 336.* Limiting instructions, like those used in the Carrs' sentencing proceeding, "often will suffice to cure any risk of prejudice." *Zafiro, supra, at 539, 113 S. Ct. 933, 122 L. Ed. 2d 317* (citing *Richardson, supra, at 211, 107 S. Ct. 1702, 95 L. Ed. 2d 176*). To forbid joinder in capital-sentencing proceedings would, perversely, *increase* the odds of "wanto[n] and freakis[h]" imposition of death sentences. *Gregg v. Georgia, 428 U. S. 153, 206-207, 96 S. Ct. 2909, 49 L. Ed. 2d 859 (1976)* (joint opinion of Stewart, Powell, and Stevens, JJ.). Better that two defendants who have together committed the same crimes be placed side-by-side to have their fates determined by a single jury.

It is improper to vacate a death sentence based on pure "speculation" of fundamental unfairness, "rather than reasoned judgment," *Romano, supra, at 13-14, 114 S. Ct. 2004, 129 L. Ed. 2d 1.* Only the most extravagant speculation would lead to the conclusion that the supposedly prejudicial evidence rendered the Carr brothers' joint sentencing proceeding fundamentally unfair. It is beyond reason to think that the jury's death verdicts were caused by the identification of Reginald as the "corrupter" or of Jonathan as the "corrupted," the jury's viewing of Reginald's handcuffs, or the sister's retracted statement that Reginald fired the final shots. None of that mattered. What these defendants did—acts of almost inconceivable cruelty and depravity—was described in excruciating detail by Holly, who relived with the jury, for two days, the Wichita Massacre. The joint sentencing proceedings did not render the sentencing proceedings fundamentally unfair.

IV

When we granted the State's petition for a writ of certiorari for the Carrs' cases, we declined to review whether the *Confrontation Clause, U. S. Const., Amdt. 6,* requires that defendants be allowed to cross-examine witnesses whose statements are recorded in police reports referred to by the State in penalty-phase proceedings. The Kansas Supreme Court did not make the admission of those statements a basis for its vacating of the death sentences, but merely "caution[ed]" that in the resentencing proceedings these out-of-court testimonial statements should be omitted, *300 Kan., at 288, 331 P. 3d, at 724.* We are confident that cross-examination regarding these police reports would not have had the slightest effect upon the sentences. See *Delaware v. Van Arsdall, 475 U. S. 673, 684, 106 S. Ct. 1431, 89 L. Ed. 2d 674 (1986).*

***

The judgments of the Supreme Court of Kansas are reversed, and these cases are remanded for further proceedings not inconsistent with this opinion.

It is so ordered.

Montgomery v. Louisiana

Supreme Court of the United States
October 13, 2015, Argued
January 25, 2016, Decided
No. 14-280
136 S. Ct. 758

HENRY MONTGOMERY,
PETITIONER
v.
LOUISIANA

Mark D. Plaisance argued the cause for petitioner.
Michael R. Dreeben argued the cause for United States, as amicus curiae, by special leave of court.
George S. Coakley argued the cause for respondents.

KENNEDY, J., delivered the opinion of the Court, in which ROBERTS, C. J., and GINSBURG, BREYER, SOTOMAYOR, and KAGAN, JJ., joined. SCALIA, J., filed a dissenting opinion, in which THOMAS and ALITO, JJ., joined. THOMAS, J., filed a dissenting opinion.

6-3 Decision; 2 Dissents.

Reversed and remanded.

JUSTICE SCALIA, with whom JUSTICE THOMAS and JUSTICE ALITO join, dissenting.

The Court has no jurisdiction to decide this case, and the decision it arrives at is wrong. I respectfully dissent.

I. Jurisdiction

Louisiana postconviction courts willingly entertain *Eighth Amendment* claims but, with limited exceptions, apply the law as it existed when the state prisoner was convicted and sentenced. Shortly after this Court announced *Teague v. Lane, 489 U. S. 288, 109 S. Ct. 1060, 103 L. Ed. 2d 334 (1989)*, the Louisiana Supreme Court adopted *Teague*'s framework to govern the provision of postconviction remedies available to *state* prisoners in its *state* courts as a matter of *state* law. *Taylor v. Whitley, 606 So. 2d 1292 (1992)*. In doing so, the court stated that it was "not bound" to adopt that federal framework. *Id., at 1296.* One would think, then, that it is none of our business that a 69-year-old Louisiana prisoner's state-law motion to be resentenced according to *Miller v. Alabama, 567 U. S. ___, 132 S. Ct. 2455, 183 L. Ed. 2d 407 (2012)*, a case announced almost half a century after his sentence was final, was met with a firm rejection on state-law grounds by the Louisiana Supreme Court. But a majority of this Court, eager to reach the merits of this case, resolves the question of our jurisdiction by deciding that the Constitution *requires* state postconviction courts to adopt *Teague*'s exception for so-called "substantive" new rules and to provide state-law remedies for the violations of those rules to prisoners whose sentences long ago became final. This conscription into federal service of state postconviction courts is nothing short of astonishing.

A

Teague announced that federal courts could not grant habeas corpus to overturn state convictions on the basis of a "new rule" of constitutional law—meaning one announced after the convictions became final—*unless* that new rule was a "substantive rule" or a "watershed rul[e] of criminal procedure." *489 U. S., at 311, 109 S. Ct. 1060, 103 L. Ed. 2d 334.* The *Teague* prescription followed from Justice Harlan's view of the "retroactivity problem" detailed in his separate opinion in *Desist v. United States, 394 U. S. 244, 256, 89 S. Ct. 1030, 22 L. Ed. 2d 248 (1969)* (dissenting opinion), and later in *Mackey v. United States, 401 U. S. 667, 675, 91 S. Ct. 1160, 28 L. Ed. 2d 404 (1971)* (opinion concurring in judgment in part and dissenting in part). Placing the rule's first exception in context requires more analysis than the majority has applied.

The Court in the mid-20th century was confounded by what Justice Harlan called the "swift pace of constitutional change," *Pickelsimer v. Wainwright, 375 U. S. 2, 4, 84 S. Ct. 80, 11 L. Ed. 2d 41 (1963)* (dissenting opinion), as it vacated and remanded many cases in the wake of *Gideon v. Wainwright, 372 U. S. 335, 83 S. Ct. 792, 9 L. Ed. 2d 799 (1963)*. Justice Harlan called upon the Court to engage in "informed and deliberate consideration" of "whether the States are constitutionally required to apply [*Gideon*'s] new rule retrospectively, which may well require the reopening of cases long since finally adjudicated in accordance with then applicable decisions of this Court." *Pickelsimer, supra, at 3, 84 S. Ct. 80, 11 L. Ed. 2d 41*. The Court answered that call in *Linkletter v. Walker, 381 U. S. 618, 85 S. Ct. 1731, 14 L. Ed. 2d 601 (1965)*. *Linkletter* began with the premise "that we are neither required to apply, nor prohibited from applying, a decision retrospectively" and went on to adopt an equitable rule-by-rule approach to retroactivity, considering "the prior history of the rule in question, its purpose and effect, and whether retrospective operation will further or retard its operation." *Id., at 629, 85 S. Ct. 1731, 14 L. Ed. 2d 601*.

The *Linkletter* framework proved unworkable when the Court began applying the rule-by-rule approach not only to cases on collateral review but also to cases on direct review, rejecting any distinction "between convictions now final" and "convictions at various stages of trial and direct review." *Stovall v. Denno, 388 U. S. 293, 300, 87 S. Ct. 1967, 18 L. Ed. 2d 1199 (1967)*. It was this rejection that drew Justice Harlan's reproach in *Desist* and later in *Mackey*. He urged that "all 'new' rules of constitutional law must, at a minimum, be applied to all those cases which are still subject to direct review by this Court at the time the 'new' decision is handed down." *Desist, supra, at 258, 89 S. Ct. 1030, 22 L. Ed. 2d 248* (dissenting opinion). "Simply fishing one case from the stream of appellate review, using it as a vehicle for pronouncing new constitutional standards, and then permitting a stream of similar cases subsequently to flow by unaffected by that new rule constitute an indefensible departure from th[e] model of judicial review." *Mackey, supra, at 679, 91 S. Ct. 1160, 28 L. Ed. 2d 404.*

The decision in *Griffith v. Kentucky, 479 U. S. 314, 107 S. Ct. 708, 93 L. Ed. 2d 649 (1987)*, heeded this constitutional concern. The Court jettisoned the *Linkletter* test for cases pending on direct review and adopted for them Justice Harlan's rule of redressability: "[F]ailure to apply a newly declared constitutional rule to criminal cases pending on direct review violates basic norms of *constitutional* adjudication." *479 U. S., at 322, 107 S. Ct. 708, 93 L. Ed. 2d 649* (emphasis added). We established in *Griffith* that this Court must play by our own "old rules"—rules we have settled before the defendant's conviction and sentence become final, even those that are a "clear break from existing precedent"—for cases pending before us on direct appeal. *Id., at 323, 107 S. Ct. 708, 93 L. Ed. 2d 649.* Since the *Griffith* rule is constitutionally compelled, we instructed the lower state and federal courts to comply with it as well. *Ibid.*

When *Teague* followed on *Griffith*'s heels two years later, the opinion contained no discussion of "basic norms of constitutional adjudication," *Griffith, supra, at 322, 107 S. Ct. 708, 93 L. Ed. 2d 649*, nor any discussion of the obligations of state courts. Doing away with *Linkletter* for good, the Court adopted Justice Harlan's solution to "the retroactivity problem" for cases pending on collateral review—which he described not as a constitutional problem but as "a problem as to the *scope of the habeas writ*." *Mackey, supra, at 684, 91 S. Ct. 1160, 28 L. Ed. 2d 404* (emphasis added). *Teague* held that federal habeas courts could no longer upset state-court convictions for violations of so-called "new rules," not yet announced when the conviction became final. *489 U. S., at 310, 109 S. Ct. 1060, 103 L. Ed. 2d 334.* But it allowed for the previously mentioned exceptions to this rule of nonredressability: substantive rules placing "certain kinds of primary, private individual conduct beyond the power of the criminal law-making authority to proscribe" and "watershed rules of criminal procedure." *Id., at 311, 109 S. Ct. 1060, 103 L. Ed. 2d 334.* Then in *Penry v. Lynaugh, 492 U. S. 302, 109 S. Ct. 2934, 106 L. Ed. 2d 256 (1989)*, the Court expanded this first exception for substantive rules to embrace new rules "prohibiting a certain category of punishment for a class of defendants because of their status or offense." *Id., at 330, 109 S. Ct. 2934, 106 L. Ed. 2d 256.*

Neither *Teague* nor its exceptions are constitutionally compelled. Unlike today's majority, the *Teague*-era Court understood that cases on collateral review are fundamentally different from those pending on direct review because of "considerations of finality in the judicial process." *Shea v. Louisiana, 470 U. S. 51, 59-60, 105 S. Ct. 1065, 84 L. Ed. 2d 38 (1985).* That line of finality demarcating the constitutionally required rule in *Griffith* from the habeas rule in *Teague* supplies the answer to the not-so-difficult question whether a state postconviction court must remedy the violation of a new substantive rule: No. A state court need only apply the law as it existed at the time a defendant's conviction and sentence became final. See *Griffith, supra, at 322, 107 S. Ct. 708, 93 L. Ed. 2d 649.* And once final, "a new rule cannot reopen a door already closed." *James B. Beam Distilling Co. v. Georgia, 501 U. S. 529, 541, 111 S. Ct. 2439, 115 L. Ed. 2d 481 (1991)* (opinion of Souter, J.). Any relief a prisoner might receive in a state court after finality is a matter of grace, not constitutional prescription.

B

The majority can marshal no case support for its contrary position. It creates a constitutional rule where none had been before: "*Teague*'s conclusion establishing the retroactivity of new substantive rules is best understood as resting upon constitutional premises" binding in both federal and state courts. *Ante,* at 8. "Best understood." Because of what? Surely not because of its history and derivation.

Because of the Supremacy Clause, says the majority. *Ante,* at 12. But the Supremacy Clause cannot possibly answer the question before us here. It only elicits another question: What federal law is supreme? Old or new? The majority's champion, Justice Harlan, said the old rules apply for federal habeas review of a state-court conviction: "[T]he habeas court need only apply the constitutional standards that prevailed at the time the original proceedings took place," *Desist, 394 U. S., at 263, 89 S. Ct. 1030, 22 L. Ed. 2d 248* (dissenting opinion), for a state court cannot "toe the constitutional mark" that does not yet exist, *Mackey, 401 U. S., at 687, 91 S. Ct. 1160, 28 L. Ed. 2d 404* (opinion of Harlan, J.). Following his analysis, we have clarified time and again—recently in *Greene v. Fisher, 565 U. S. ___, ___-___, 132 S. Ct. 38, 181 L. Ed. 2d 336 (2011) (slip op., at 4-5)*—that *federal* habeas courts are to review state-court decisions against the law and factual record that existed at the time the decisions were made. "*Section 2254(d)(1)* [of the federal habeas statute] refers, in the past tense, to a state-court adjudication that 'resulted in' a decision that was contrary to, or 'involved' an unreasonable application of, established law. This backward-looking language requires an examination of the state-court decision at the time it was made." *Cullen v. Pinholster, 563 U. S. 170, 181-182, 131 S. Ct. 1388, 179 L. Ed. 2d 557 (2011).* How can it possibly be, then, that the Constitution requires a *state* court's review of its own convictions to be governed by "new rules" rather than (what suffices when federal courts review state courts) "old rules"?

The majority relies on the statement in *United States v. United States Coin & Currency, 401 U. S. 715, 91 S. Ct. 1041, 28 L. Ed. 2d 434 (1971),* that "'[n]o circumstances call more for the invocation of a rule of complete retroactivity'" than when "'the conduct being penalized is constitutionally immune from punishment.'" *Ante,* at 9-10 (quoting *401 U. S., at 724, 91 S. Ct. 1041, 28 L. Ed. 2d 434*). The majority neglects to mention that this statement was addressing the "circumstances" of a conviction that "had *not become final," id.,* at 724, n. 13, 91 S. Ct. 1041, 28 L. Ed. 2d 434 (emphasis added), when the "rule of complete retroactivity" was invoked. *Coin & Currency,* an opinion written by (guess whom?) Justice Harlan, merely foreshadowed the rule announced in *Griffith,* that all cases pending on direct review receive the benefit of newly announced rules—better termed "old rules" for such rules were announced *before* finality.

The majority also misappropriates *Yates v. Aiken, 484 U. S. 211, 108 S. Ct. 534, 98 L. Ed. 2d 546 (1988),* which reviewed a state habeas petitioner's *Fourteenth Amendment* claim that the jury instructions at his trial lessened the State's burden to prove every element of his offense beyond a reasonable doubt. That case at least did involve a conviction that was final. But the majority is oblivious to the critical fact that Yates's claim depended upon an *old rule,* settled at the time of his trial. *Id.,* at 217, 108 S. Ct. 534, 98 L. Ed. 2d 546. This Court reversed the state habeas court for its refusal to consider that the jury instructions violated that *old rule. Ibid.* The majority places great weight upon the dictum in *Yates* that the South Carolina habeas court "'ha[d] a duty to grant the relief that federal law requires.'" *Ante,* at 13 (quoting *Yates, supra,* at 218, 108 S. Ct. 534, 98 L. Ed. 2d 546). It is simply wrong to divorce that dictum from the facts it addressed. In that context, *Yates* merely reinforces the line drawn by *Griffith*: when state courts provide a forum for postconviction relief, they need to play by the "old rules" announced *before* the date on which a defendant's conviction and sentence became final.

The other sleight of hand performed by the majority is its emphasis on *Ex parte Siebold, 100 U. S. 371, 25 L. Ed. 717 (1880)*. That case considered a petition for a federal writ of habeas corpus following a federal conviction, and the initial issue it confronted was its jurisdiction. A federal court has no inherent habeas corpus power, *Ex parte Bollman, 8 U.S. 75, 4 Cranch 75, 94, 2 L. Ed. 554 (1807)*, but only that which is conferred (and limited) by statute, see, *e.g., Felker v. Turpin, 518 U. S. 651, 664, 116 S. Ct. 2333, 135 L. Ed. 2d 827 (1996)*. As *Siebold* stated, it was forbidden to use the federal habeas writ "as a mere writ of error." *100 U. S., at 375, 25 L. Ed. 717* . "The only ground on which this court, or any court, without some special statute authorizing it, [could] give relief on *habeas corpus* to a prisoner under conviction and sentence of another court is the want of jurisdiction in such court over the person or the cause, or some other matter rendering its proceedings void." *Ibid.* Turning to the facts before it, the Court decided it was within its power to hear Siebold's claim, which did not merely protest that the conviction and sentence were "erroneous" but contended that the statute he was convicted of violating was unconstitutional and the conviction therefore void: "[I]f the laws are unconstitutional and void, the Circuit Court acquired no jurisdiction of the causes." *Id., at 376-377, 25 L. Ed. 717*. *Siebold* is thus a decision that expands the limits of this Court's power to issue a federal habeas writ for a federal prisoner.

The majority, however, divines from *Siebold* "a general principle" that "a court has no authority to leave in place a conviction or sentence that violates a substantive rule, regardless of whether the conviction or sentence became final before the rule was announced." *Ante*, at 11. That is utterly impossible. No "general principle" can rationally be derived from *Siebold* about constitutionally required remedies in state courts; indeed, the opinion does not even speak to constitutionally required remedies in *federal* courts. It is a decision about this Court's statutory power to grant the Original Writ, not about its constitutional obligation to do so. Nowhere in *Siebold* did this Court intimate that relief was constitutionally required—or as the majority puts it, that a court would have had "no authority" to leave in place Siebold's conviction, *ante,* at 11.

The majority's sorry acknowledgment that "*Siebold* and the other cases discussed in this opinion, of course, do not directly control the question the Court now answers for the first time," *ibid.,* is not nearly enough of a disclaimer. It is not just that they "do not directly control," but that the dicta cherry picked from those cases are irrelevant; they addressed circumstances fundamentally different from those to which the majority now applies them. Indeed, we know for sure that the author of some of those dicta, Justice Harlan, held views that flatly contradict the majority.

The majority's maxim that "state collateral review courts have no greater power than federal habeas courts to mandate that a prisoner continue to suffer punishment barred by the Constitution," *ante,* at 12-13, begs the question rather than contributes to its solution. Until today, no federal court was *constitutionally obliged* to grant relief for the past violation of a newly announced substantive rule. Until today, it was Congress's prerogative to do away with *Teague*'s exceptions altogether. Indeed, we had left unresolved the question whether Congress had already done that when it amended a section of the habeas corpus statute to add backward-looking language governing the review of state-court decisions. See Antiterrorism and Effective Death Penalty Act of 1996, §104, 110 Stat. 1219, codified at *28 U. S. C. §2254(d)(1)*; *Greene, 565 U. S, at ___, 132 S. Ct. 38, 181 L. Ed. 2d 336*, n. (slip op., at 5, n.). A maxim shown to be more relevant to this case, by the analysis that the majority omitted, is this: The Supremacy Clause does not impose upon state courts a constitutional obligation it fails to impose upon federal courts.

C

All that remains to support the majority's conclusion is that all-purpose Latin canon: *ipse dixit.* The majority opines that because a substantive rule eliminates a State's power to proscribe certain conduct or impose a certain punishment, it has "the automatic consequence of invalidating a defendant's conviction or sentence." *Ante,* at 9. What provision of the Constitution could conceivably produce such a result? The *Due Process Clause*? It surely cannot be a denial of due process for a court to pronounce a final judgment which, though fully in accord with federal constitutional law at the time, fails to anticipate a change to be made by this Court half a century into the future. The *Equal Protection Clause?* Both statutory and (increasingly) constitutional laws change. If it were a denial of equal protection to hold an earlier defendant to a law more stringent than what exists today, it would also be a denial of equal protection to hold a later defendant to a law more stringent than what existed 50 years ago. No principle of equal protection requires the criminal law of all ages to be the same.

The majority grandly asserts that "[t]here is no grandfather clause that permits States to *enforce punishments the Constitution forbids.*" *Ante*, at 12 (emphasis added). Of course the italicized phrase begs the question. There most certainly is a grandfather clause—one we have called *finality*—which says that the Constitution does not require States to revise punishments that were lawful when they were imposed. Once a conviction has become final, whether new rules or old ones will be applied to revisit the conviction is a matter entirely within the State's control; the Constitution has nothing to say about that choice. The majority says that there is no "possibility of a valid result" when a new substantive rule is not applied retroactively. *Ante*, at 9. But the whole controversy here arises because many think there *is* a valid result when a defendant has been convicted under the law that existed when his conviction became final. And the States are unquestionably entitled to take that view of things.

The majority's imposition of *Teague*'s first exception upon the States is all the worse because it does not adhere to that exception as initially conceived by Justice Harlan—an exception for rules that "place, as a matter of constitutional interpretation, certain kinds of primary, private individual *conduct* beyond the power of the criminal lawmaking authority to proscribe." *Mackey, 401 U. S., at 692, 91 S. Ct. 1160, 28 L. Ed. 2d 404* (emphasis added). Rather, it endorses the exception as expanded by *Penry*, to include "rules prohibiting a certain category of punishment for a class of defendants because of their status or offense." *492 U. S., at 330, 109 S. Ct. 2934, 106 L. Ed. 2d 256*. That expansion empowered and obligated federal (and after today state) habeas courts to invoke this Court's *Eighth Amendment* "evolving standards of decency" jurisprudence to upset punishments that were constitutional when imposed but are "cruel and unusual," U. S. Const., Amdt. 8, in our newly enlightened society. See *Trop v. Dulles, 356 U. S. 86, 101, 78 S. Ct. 590, 2*

L. Ed. 2d 630 (1958). The "evolving standards" test concedes that in 1969 the State had the power to punish Henry Montgomery as it did. Indeed, Montgomery could at that time have been sentenced to death by our yet unevolved society. Even 20 years later, this Court reaffirmed that the Constitution posed no bar to death sentences for juveniles. *Stanford v. Kentucky, 492 U. S. 361, 109 S. Ct. 2969, 106 L. Ed. 2d 306 (1989)*. Not until our People's "standards of decency" evolved a mere 10 years ago—nearly 40 years after Montgomery's sentence was imposed—did this Court declare the death penalty unconstitutional for juveniles. *Roper v. Simmons, 543 U. S. 551, 125 S. Ct. 1183, 161 L. Ed. 2d 1 (2005)*. Even then, the Court reassured States that "the punishment of life imprisonment without the possibility of parole is itself a severe sanction," implicitly still available for juveniles. *Id., at 572, 125 S. Ct. 1183, 161 L. Ed. 2d 1*. And again five years ago this Court left in place this severe sanction for juvenile homicide offenders. *Graham v. Florida, 560 U. S. 48, 69, 130 S. Ct. 2011, 176 L. Ed. 2d 825 (2010)*. So for the five decades Montgomery has spent in prison, not one of this Court's precedents called into question the legality of his sentence—until the People's "standards of decency," as perceived by five Justices, "evolved" yet again in *Miller*.

Teague's central purpose was to do away with the old regime's tendency to *"continually* force the States to marshal resources in order to keep in prison defendants whose trials and appeals conformed to then-existing constitutional standards." *489 U. S., at 310, 109 S. Ct. 1060, 103 L. Ed. 2d 334*. Today's holding thwarts that purpose with a vengeance. Our ever-evolving Constitution changes the rules of "cruel and unusual punishments" every few years. In the passage from *Mackey* that the majority's opinion quotes, *ante*, at 13, Justice Harlan noted the diminishing force of finality (and hence the equitable propriety—not the constitutional requirement—of disregarding it) when the law punishes nonpunishable conduct, see *401 U. S., at 693, 91 S. Ct. 1160, 28 L. Ed. 2d 404*. But one cannot imagine a clearer frustration of the sensible policy of *Teague* when the ever-moving target of impermissible *punishments* is at issue. Today's holding not only forecloses Congress from eliminating this expansion of *Teague* in federal courts, but also foists this distortion upon the States.

II. The Retroactivity of *Miller*

Having created jurisdiction by ripping *Teague*'s first exception from its moorings, converting an equitable rule governing federal habeas relief to a constitutional command governing state courts as well, the majority proceeds to the merits. And here it confronts a second obstacle to its desired outcome. *Miller*, the opinion it wishes to impose upon state postconviction courts, simply does not decree what the first part of the majority's opinion says *Teague*'s first exception requires to be given retroactive effect: a rule "set[ting] forth *categorical* constitutional guarantees that place certain criminal laws and punishments *altogether* beyond the State's power to impose." *Ante*, at 9 (emphasis added). No problem. Having distorted *Teague*, the majority simply proceeds to rewrite *Miller*.

The majority asserts that *Miller* "rendered life without parole an unconstitutional penalty for 'a class of defendants because of their status'—that is, juvenile offenders whose crimes reflect the transient immaturity of youth." *Ante*, at 17. It insists that *Miller* barred life-without-parole sentences "for all but the rarest of juvenile offenders, those whose crimes reflect permanent incorrigibility. For that reason, *Miller* is no less substantive than are *Roper* and *Graham*." *Ante*, at 17-18. The problem is that *Miller* stated, quite clearly, precisely the opposite: "Our decision does not categorically bar a penalty for a class of offenders or type of crime—as, for example, we did in *Roper* or *Graham*. Instead, it mandates only that a sentencer *follow a certain process*—considering an offender's youth and attendant characteristics—before imposing a particular penalty." *567 U. S., at ___, 132 S. Ct. 2455, 2472, 183 L. Ed. 2d 407, 427* (emphasis added).

To contradict that clear statement, the majority opinion quotes passages from *Miller* that assert such things as "mandatory life-without-parole sentences for children 'pos[e] too great a risk of disproportionate punishment'" and "'appropriate occasions for sentencing juveniles to this harshest possible penalty will be uncommon.'" *Ante*, at 16 (quoting *Miller, supra, at ___, 132 S. Ct. 2455, 2481, 183 L. Ed. 2d 407, 437*). But to say that a punishment might be inappropriate and disproportionate for certain juvenile offenders is not to say that it is unconstitutionally void. All of the statements relied on by the majority do nothing more than express the *reason* why the new, youth-protective *procedure* prescribed by *Miller* is desirable: to deter life sentences for certain juvenile offenders. On the issue of whether *Miller* rendered life-without-parole penalties unconstitutional, it is impossible to get past *Miller*'s unambiguous statement that "[o]ur decision does not categorically bar a penalty for a class of offenders" and "mandates only that a sentencer follow a certain process . . . before imposing a particular penalty." *567 U. S., at ___, 132 S. Ct. 2455, 2471, 183 L. Ed. 2d 407, 426.* It is plain as day that the majority is not applying *Miller*, but rewriting it. [1]

And the rewriting has consequences beyond merely making *Miller*'s procedural guarantee retroactive. If, indeed, a State is categorically prohibited from imposing life without parole on juvenile offenders whose crimes do not "reflect permanent incorrigibility," then even when the procedures that *Miller* demands are provided the constitutional requirement is not necessarily satisfied. It remains available for the defendant sentenced to life without parole to argue that his crimes did not in fact "reflect permanent incorrigibility." Or as the majority's opinion puts it: "That *Miller* did not impose a formal factfinding requirement does not leave States free to sentence a child[[2]] whose crime reflects transient immaturity to life without parole. To the contrary, *Miller* established that this punishment is disproportionate under the *Eighth Amendment.*" *Ante*, at 20.

How wonderful. Federal and (like it or not) state judges are henceforth to resolve the knotty "legal" question: whether a 17-year-old who murdered an innocent sheriff's deputy half a century ago was at the time of his trial "incorrigible." Under *Miller*, bear in mind, the inquiry is whether the inmate was seen to be incorrigible when he was sentenced—not whether he has proven corrigible and so can safely be paroled today. What silliness. (And how impossible in practice, see Brief for National District Attorneys Assn. et al. as *Amici Curiae* 9-17.) When in *Lockett v. Ohio, 438 U. S. 586, 608, 98 S. Ct. 2954, 57 L. Ed. 2d 973 (1978)*, the Court imposed the thitherto unheard-of requirement

---

[1] It is amusing that the majority's initial description of *Miller* is the same as our own: "[T]he Court held that a juvenile convicted of a homicide offense could not be sentenced to life in prison without parole absent consideration of the juvenile's special circumstances in light of the principles and purposes of juvenile sentencing." *Ante*, at 1. Only 15 pages later, after softening the reader with 3 pages of obfuscating analysis, does the majority dare to attribute to *Miller* that which *Miller* explicitly denies.

[2] The majority presumably regards any person one day short of voting age as a "child."

that the sentencer in capital cases must consider and weigh all "relevant mitigating factors," it at least did not impose the substantive (and hence judicially reviewable) requirement that the aggravators must outweigh the mitigators; it would suffice that the sentencer *thought* so. And, fairly read, *Miller* did the same. Not so with the "incorrigibility" requirement that the Court imposes today to make *Miller* retroactive.

But have no fear. The majority does not seriously expect state and federal collateral-review tribunals to engage in this silliness, probing the evidence of "incorrigibility" that existed decades ago when defendants were sentenced. What the majority expects (and intends) to happen is set forth in the following not-so-subtle invitation: "A State may remedy a *Miller* violation by permitting juvenile homicide offenders to be considered for parole, rather than by resentencing them." *Ante*, at 21. Of course. This whole exercise, this whole distortion of *Miller*, is just a devious way of eliminating life without parole for juvenile offenders. The Court might have done that expressly (as we know, the Court can decree *anything*), but that would have been something of an embarrassment. After all, one of the justifications the Court gave for decreeing an end to the death penalty for murders (no matter how many) committed by a juvenile was that life without parole was a severe enough punishment. See *Roper, 543 U. S., at 572, 125 S. Ct. 1183, 161 L. Ed. 2d 1.* How could the majority—in an opinion written by the very author of *Roper*—now say *that* punishment is *also* unconstitutional? The Court expressly refused to say so in *Miller.* 567 U. S., at ___, 132 S. Ct. 2455, 183 L. Ed. 2d 407 (slip op., at 17). So the Court refuses again today, but merely makes imposition of that severe sanction a practical impossibility. And then, in Godfather fashion, the majority makes state legislatures an offer they can't refuse: Avoid all the utterly impossible nonsense we have prescribed by simply "permitting juvenile homicide offenders to be considered for parole." *Ante,* at 21. Mission accomplished.

FERC v. Elec. Power Supply Ass'n

Supreme Court of the United States
October 14, 2015, Argued
January 25, 2016, Decided
Nos. 14-840 and 14-841
136 S. Ct. 760

FEDERAL ENERGY REGULATORY COMMISSION,
PETITIONER
v.
ELECTRIC POWER SUPPLY ASSOCIATION, ET AL. ;

ENERNOC, INC., ET AL.,
PETITIONERS
v.
ELECTRIC POWER SUPPLY ASSOCIATION, ET AL.

Donald B. Verrilli, Jr. argued the cause for petitioner.
Carter G. Phillips argued the cause for petitioners.
Paul D. Clement argued the cause for respondents.

KAGAN, J., delivered the opinion of the Court, in which ROBERTS, C. J., and KENNEDY, GINSBURG, BREYER, and SOTOMAYOR, JJ., joined. SCALIA, J. filed a dissenting opinion, in which THOMAS, J., joined. ALITO, J., took no part in the consideration or decision of the cases.

6-2 Decision; 1 Dissent.

Reversed and remanded.

JUSTICE SCALIA, with whom JUSTICE THOMAS joins, dissenting.

I believe the Federal Power Act (FPA or Act), *16 U. S. C. §791a et seq.*, prohibits the Federal Energy Regulatory Commission (FERC) from regulating the demand response of retail purchasers of power. I respectfully dissent from the Court's holding to the contrary.

I

A

I agree with the majority that FERC has the authority to regulate practices "affecting" wholesale rates. *§§824d(a), 824e(a)*; *Mississippi Power & Light Co. v. Mississippi ex rel. Moore, 487 U. S. 354, 371, 108 S. Ct. 2428, 101 L. Ed. 2d 322 (1988)*. I also agree that this so-called "affecting" jurisdiction cannot be limitless. And I suppose I could even live with the Court's "direct effect" test as a reasonable limit. *Ante,* at 15. But as the majority recognizes, *ante,* at 17, that extratextual limit on the "affecting" jurisdiction merely supplements, not supplants, limits that are already contained in the statutory text and structure. I believe the Court misconstrues the primary statutory limit. (Like the majority, I think that deference under *Chevron U. S. A. Inc. v. Natural Resources Defense Council, Inc., 467 U. S. 837, 104 S. Ct. 2778, 81 L. Ed. 2d 694 (1984)*, is unwarranted because the statute is clear.)

The Act grants FERC authority to regulate the "generation . . . [and] transmission of electric energy in interstate commerce and the sale of such energy at wholesale." *§824(a)*. Yet the majority frames the issue thusly: "[T]o uphold the [r]ule, we also must determine that it does not regulate *retail* electricity sales." *Ante,* at 17. That formulation inverts the proper inquiry. The pertinent question under the Act is whether the rule regulates sales *"at wholesale."* If so, it falls within FERC's regulatory authority. If not, the rule is unauthorized whether or not it happens to regulate *"retail* electricity sales"; for, with exceptions not material here, the FPA prohibits FERC from regulating *"any other* sale of electric energy" that is *not* at wholesale. *§824(b)(1)* (emphasis added). (The majority wisely ignores FERC's specious argument that the demand-response rule does not regulate any sale, wholesale or retail. See Brief for Petitioner in No. 14-840, p. 39. Paying someone *not* to conclude a transaction that otherwise would without a doubt have been concluded is most assuredly a regulation of that transaction. Cf. *Gonzales v. Raich, 545 U. S. 1, 39-40, 125 S. Ct. 2195, 162 L. Ed. 2d 1 (2005)* (SCALIA, J., concurring in judgment).)

Properly framing the inquiry matters not because I think there exists "some undefined category of . . . electricity sales" that is "non-retail [and] non-wholesale," *ante,* at 18, n. 7, [1] but because a proper framing of the inquiry is important to establish the default presumption regarding the scope of FERC's authority. While the majority would find every sale of electric energy to be *within* FERC's authority to regulate *unless* the transaction is demonstrably a retail sale, the statute actually *excludes* from FERC's jurisdiction all sales of electric energy *except* those that are demonstrably sales at wholesale.

So what, exactly, is a "sale of electric energy at wholesale"? We need not guess, for the Act provides a definition: "a sale of electric energy to any person *for resale.*" *§824(d)* (emphasis added). No matter how many times the majority incants and italicizes the word "wholesale," *ante,* at 19-20, nothing can change the fact that the vast majority of (and likely all) demand-response participants — "[a]ggregators of multiple users of electricity, as well as large-scale individual users like factories or big-box stores," *ante,* at 7—*do not resell electric energy;* they consume it themselves. FERC's own definition of demand response is aimed at energy *consumers,* not resellers. *18 CFR §35.28(b)(4) (2015).*

It is therefore quite beside the point that the challenged "[r]ule addresses — and addresses only — transactions occurring on the wholesale market," *ante,* at 19. For FERC's regulatory authority over electric-energy sales depends not on which "market" the "transactions occu[r] on" (whatever that means), but rather on the *identity of the putative purchaser.* If the purchaser is one who resells electric energy to other customers, the transaction is one "at wholesale" and thus within FERC's authority. If not, then not. Or so, at least, says the statute. As we long ago said of the parallel provision in the Natural Gas Act, *15 U. S. C. §717,* "[t]he line of the statute [i]s thus clear and complete. It

---

[1] Although the majority dismisses this possibility, in fact it appears to think that demand response is in that category: It rejects the conclusion that the demand-response rule regulates retail sales, *ante,* at 17-23, yet also implicitly rejects the conclusion that it regulates wholesale sales—otherwise why rely on FERC's "affecting" jurisdiction to rescue the rule's legitimacy?

cut[s] sharply and cleanly between sales for resale and direct sales for consumptive uses. No exceptions [a]re made in either category for particular uses, quantities, or otherwise." *Panhandle Eastern Pipe Line Co. v. Public Serv. Comm'n of Ind., 332 U.S. 507, 517, 68 S. Ct. 190, 92 L. Ed. 128 (1947).* The majority makes no textual response to this plain reading of the statute.

The demand-response bidders here indisputably do not resell energy to other customers. It follows that the rule does not regulate electric-energy sales "at wholesale," and *16 U. S. C. §824(b)(1)* therefore forbids FERC to regulate these demand-response transactions. See *New York v. FERC, 535 U. S. 1, 17, 122 S. Ct. 1012, 152 L. Ed. 2d 47 (2002).* That is so whether or not those transactions "directly affect" wholesale rates; as we recently said in another context, we will not adopt a construction that "needlessly produces a contradiction in the statutory text." *Shapiro v. McManus, 577 U. S. ___, ___, 136 S. Ct. 450, 193 L. Ed. 2d 279, 284 (2015).* A faithful application of that principle would compel the conclusion that FERC may not "do under *[§§824d(a)* and *824e(a)]* what [it] is forbidden to do under *[§824(b)(1)]." Id.,* at ___, *136 S. Ct. 450, 193 L. Ed. 2d 279, 285.*

B

The analysis could stop there. But the majority is wrong even on its own terms, for the rule at issue here does in fact regulate "*retail* electricity sales," which are indisputably "matters . . . subject to regulation by the States" and therefore off-limits to FERC. *§824(a);* see *FPC v. Conway Corp., 426 U. S. 271, 276, 96 S. Ct. 1999, 48 L. Ed. 2d 626 (1976); Panhandle Eastern Pipe Line Co., supra,* at *517-518, 68 S. Ct. 190, 92 L. Ed. 2d 128.* The demand-response participants are retail customers — they purchase electric energy solely for their own consumption. And FERC's demand-response scheme is intentionally "designed to induce lower consumption of electric energy" — in other words, to induce a reduction in "*retail* electricity sales" — by offering "incentive payments" to those customers. *18 CFR §35.28(b)(4).* The incentive payments effectively increase the retail price of electric energy for participating customers because they must now account for the opportunity cost of using, as opposed to abstaining from using, more energy. In other words, it literally *costs them more* to buy energy on the retail market. In the court below, FERC conceded that offering *credits* to retail customers to reduce their electricity consumption "would be an impermissible intrusion into the retail market" because it would in effect regulate retail rates. *753 F. 3d 216, 223, 410 U.S. App. D.C. 103 (CADC 2014).* Demand-response incentive payments are identical in substance.

The majority resists this elementary economic conclusion (notwithstanding its own exhortation to "think back to Econ 101," *ante*, at 5). Why? Because its self-proclaimed "common-sensical" view dictates otherwise. *Ante*, at 22. Maybe the easiest way to see the majority's error is to take its own example: an airline passenger who rejects a $300 voucher for taking a later flight. Consider the following formulation of that example, indistinguishable in substance from the majority's formulation. (Indistinguishable because the hypothetical passenger has exactly the same options and outcomes available to him.) Suppose the airline said to the passenger: "We have proactively canceled your ticket and refunded $400 to your account; and because we have inconvenienced you, we have also deposited an extra $300. The money is yours to use as you like. But if you insist on repurchasing a ticket on the same flight, you must not only pay us $400, but return the $300 too." *Now* what is the effective price of the ticket? Sometimes an allegedly commonsensical intuition is just that — an intuition, often mistaken.

Moving closer to home, recall that demand-response participants must choose either to purchase a unit of energy at the prevailing retail price (say $10) or to withhold from purchasing that unit and receive instead an incentive payment (of say $5). The two options thus present a choice between having a unit of energy, on the one hand, and having $15 more in the bank, on the other. To repeat: take the energy, be $15 poorer; forgo the energy, be $15 richer. Is that not the very definition of price? See Black's Law Dictionary 1380 (10th ed. 2014) ("[t]he amount of money or other consideration asked for or given in exchange for something else"). In fact, is that not *the majority's* definition of price? *Ante*, at 21 ("the amount of money a consumer will hand over in exchange for power").

In any event, the majority appears to recognize that the effective price is indeed $15 — just as the effective price of the airline ticket in the hypothetical is $700. *Ante*, at 22-23, n. 9. That recognition gives away the game. For FERC is prohibited not just from directly setting or modifying retail *prices*; it is prohibited from regulating retail *sales*, no matter the means. *Panhandle Eastern Pipe Line Co., supra,* at 517, 68 S. Ct. 190, 92 L. Ed. 2d 128. Whether FERC sets the "real" retail price (to use the majority's idiosyncratic terminology, *ante,* at 23, n. 9) or the "effective" retail price is immaterial; either way, the rule—*by design*—induces demand-response participants to forgo retail electric-energy purchases they otherwise would have made. As noted, even FERC conceded that offering credits to retail customers would impermissibly regulate retail sales. The majority blithely overlooks this concession in favor of its own my-opic view of retail pricing—all the while evading the incon-venient fact that fiddling with the effective retail price of electric energy, be it through incentive payments or hypothetical credits, *regulates retail sales* of electric energy no less than does direct ratesetting.

C

The majority cites dicta in several of our opinions expressing the assumption that state jurisdiction and federal jurisdiction under FERC cover the field, so that there is no regulatory "gap"; one entity or the other "must have jurisdiction to regulate each and every practice that takes place in the electricity markets." *Ante,* at 27. The cases that express such a principle, with respect to the Federal Power Act and its companion the Natural Gas Act, base it (no surprise) on legislative history. See, *e.g., FPC v. Louisiana Power & Light Co.,* 406 U. S. 621, 631, 92 S. Ct. 1827, 32 L. Ed. 2d 369 (1972); *FPC v. Transcontinental Gas Pipe Line Corp.,* 365 U. S. 1, 19, 81 S. Ct. 435, 5 L. Ed. 2d 377 (1961); *Panhandle Eastern Pipe Line Co.,* 332 U. S., at 517-518, 68 S. Ct. 190, 92 L. Ed. 2d 128, and n. 13. One would *expect* the congressional proponents of legislation to assert that it is "comprehensive" and leaves no stone unturned. But even if one is a fan of legislative history, surely one cannot rely upon such generalities in determining what a statute actually *does.* Whether it is "comprehensive" and leaves not even the most minor regulatory "gap" surely depends on what it says and not on what its proponents hoped to achieve. I cannot imagine a more irrational interpretive principle than the following, upon which the majority evidently relies:

> "[W]hen a dispute arises over whether a given transaction is within the scope of federal or state regulatory authority, we are not inclined to approach the problem negatively, thus raising the

possibility that a 'no man's land' will be created. That is to say, in a borderline case where congressional authority is not explicit we must ask whether state authority can practicably regulate a given area and, if we find that it cannot, then we are impelled to decide that federal authority governs." *Transcontinental Gas Pipe Line Corp., supra, at 19-20, 81 S. Ct. 435, 5 L. Ed. 2d 377* (citation omitted).

That extravagant and otherwise-unheard-of method of establishing regulatory jurisdiction was not necessary to the judgments that invoked it, and should disappear in the Court's memory hole.

Suppose FERC decides that eliminating the middleman would benefit the public, and therefore promulgates a rule allowing electric-energy generators to sell directly to retail consumers across state lines and fixing generation, transmission, and retail rates for such sales. I think it obvious this hypothetical scheme would be forbidden to FERC. Yet just as surely the States could not enact it either, for only FERC has authority to regulate "the transmission of electric energy in interstate commerce." *16 U. S. C. §824(b)(1)*; see also *New York, 535 U. S., at 19-20, 122 S. Ct. 1012, 152 L. Ed. 2d 47.* Is this a regulatory "gap"? Has the generator-to-consumer sales scheme fallen into a regulatory "no man's land"? *Must* FERC therefore be allowed to implement this scheme on its own? Applying the majority's *logic* would yield nothing but "yesses." Yet the majority acknowledges that neither FERC nor the States have regulatory jurisdiction over this scheme. *Ante,* at 27, n. 10. Such sales transactions, involving a mix of retail and wholesale players — *as the demand-response scheme does*—can be regulated (if at all) only by joint action. I would not call that a "problem," *ante,* at 26; I would call it an inevitable consequence of the federal-state division created by the FPA.

The majority is evidently distraught that affirming the decision below "would . . . extinguish the wholesale demand response program in its entirety." *Ante,* at 27. Alarmist hyperbole. Excluding FERC jurisdiction would at most eliminate *this particular flavor* of FERC-regulated demand response. Nothing prevents FERC from tweaking its demand-response scheme by requiring incentive payments to be offered to *wholesale* customers, rather than retail ones. Brief for Respondent Electric Power Supply Assn. (EPSA) et al. 47-48; Brief for Respondents Midwest Load-Serving Entities 10-11. And retail-level demand-response programs, run by the States, do and would continue to exist. See Brief for Respondent EPSA et al. 46-47; Brief for Respondents Midwest Load-Serving Entities 6-11. In fact Congress seemed to presuppose that *States*, not FERC, would run such programs: The relevant provisions of the Energy Policy Act of 2005, 119 Stat. 594 *et seq*, are intended "to encourage *States* to coordinate, on a regional basis, *State* energy policies to provide reliable and affordable demand response services." §1252(e)(1), *id.*, at 965, codified at *16 U. S. C. §2642* note (emphasis added). That statute also imposes several duties on the Secretary of Energy to assist States in implementing demand-response programs. §§1252(e)(2), (e)(3), 119 Stat. 965-966. In context, §1252(f) of the 2005 Act is therefore best read as directing the Secretary to eliminate "unnecessary barriers" to *States'* adopting and implementing demand-response systems — and not, as the majority contends, as "praising *wholesale* demand response" systems to be deployed and regulated by FERC, *ante*, at 9 (emphasis added).

Moreover, the rule itself allows States to forbid their retail customers to participate in the existing demand-response scheme. *18 CFR §35.28(g)(1)(i)(A)*; see Brief for Petitioner in No. 14-840, at 43. The majority accepts FERC's argument that this is merely a matter of grace, and claims that it puts the "finishing blow" to respondents' argument that *16 U. S. C. §824(b)(1)* prohibits the scheme. *Ante*, at 25. Quite the contrary. Remember that the majority believes FERC's authority derives from *16 U. S. C. §§824d(a)* and *824e(a)*, the grants of "affecting" jurisdiction. Yet those provisions impose a *duty* on FERC to ensure that "all rules and regulations affecting or pertaining to [wholesale] rates or charges *shall be just and reasonable.*" *§824d(a)* (emphasis added); see *§824e(a)* (similar); *Conway Corp., 426 U. S., at 277-279, 96 S. Ct. 1999, 48 L. Ed. 2d 626.* If inducing retail customers to participate in wholesale demand-response transactions is necessary to render wholesale rates "just and reasonable," how can FERC, consistent with its statutory mandate, permit States to thwart such participation? See Brief for United States as *Amicus Curiae* 20-21, in *Hughes* v. *Talen Energy Marketing, LLC*, No. 14-614 etc., now pending before the Court (making an argument similar to ours); cf. *New England Power Co. v. New Hampshire, 455 U. S. 331, 339-341, 102 S. Ct. 1096, 71 L. Ed. 2d 188 (1982).* Although not legally relevant, the fact that FERC—ordinarily so jealous of its regulatory authority, see Brief for United States as *Amicus Curiae* in No. 14-614 etc.—is willing to let States opt out of its demand-response scheme serves to highlight just how far the rule intrudes into the retail electricity market.

II

Having found the rule to be within FERC's authority, the Court goes on to hold that FERC's choice of compensating demand-response bidders with the "locational marginal price" is not arbitrary and capricious. There are strong arguments that it is. Brief for Robert L. Borlick et al. as *Amici Curiae* 5-34. Since, however, I believe FERC's rule is ultra vires I have neither need nor desire to analyze whether, if it were not ultra vires, it would be reasonable.

***

For the foregoing reasons, I respectfully dissent.

Other orders with Scalia's name from the 2015 Term and 136th volume of West's Supreme Court Reporter:

GUSTAVO J. GARCIA, v. STEPHENS, DIR., TX DCJ.

No. 15-6557.

February 10, 2016.

The application for stay of execution of sentence of death presented to Justice Scalia and by him referred to the Court is denied. The petition for rehearing is denied.

WILLIAM A. GUTIERREZ, v. UNITED STATES.

No. 15A795.

February 3, 2016.

The application for stay of surrender and extradition presented to Justice Scalia and by him referred to the Court is denied.

SIDNEY BENDER, v. OBAMA, PRESIDENT OF U.S., ET AL.

No. 15A567.

January 11, 2016.

The application for a temporary injunction pending the disposition of the petition for a writ of certiorari addressed to Justice Scalia and referred to the Court is denied.

136 S.Ct. 387 (2015)

Raphael Deon HOLIDAY, v. William STEPHENS, Director, Texas Department of Criminal Justice, Correctional Institutions Division.

No. 15-6956 (15A520).

November 18, 2015.

The application for stay of execution of sentence of death presented to Justice SCALIA and by him referred to the Court is denied. The petition for writ of certiorari is denied. Statement of Justice SOTOMAYOR, respecting the application for stay of execution and denial of certiorari.

136 S.Ct. 18 (2015)

Stephen DUNCAN, Warden, applicant,

v. Lawrence OWENS.

No. 15A111 (14-1516).

August 13, 2015.

Application to recall and stay the mandate pending disposition of the petition for writ of certiorari addressed to Justice SCALIA and by him referred to the Court denied.

136 S.Ct. 17 (2015)

Daniel Lee LOPEZ, applicant, v. William STEPHENS, Director, Texas Department of Criminal Justice, Correctional Institutions Division.

No. 15A48 (15-5141).

August 12, 2015.

Application for stay of execution of sentence of death presented to Justice SCALIA and by him referred to the Court denied. Motion for leave to proceed in forma pauperis and petition for writ of certiorari to the United States Court of Appeals for the Fifth Circuit denied.

Justice GINSBURG and Justice SOTOMAYOR would vote to grant the motion for leave to proceed in forma pauperis.

And also from the 2015 term, see named defendant in:

KENNETH L. SMITH, v. SCALIA, JUSTICE, USSC, ET AL.

No. 15-454.

November 30, 2015.

Because the Court lacks a quorum, 28 U. S. C. §1, and since the only qualified Justices are of the opinion that the case cannot be heard and determined at the next Term of the Court, the judgment is affirmed under 28 U. S. C. §2109, which provides that under these circumstances "the court shall enter its order affirming the judgment of the court from which the case was brought for review with the same effect as upon affirmance by an equally divided court."

CONCLUSION

This book is a collection of the writings by Justice Antonin "Nino" Scalia in his final months as Associate Justice of the U.S. Supreme Court. Terms of the U.S. Supreme Court begin the first Monday of October and Justice Scalia died on February 13, 2016, near the middle of the 2015 term. Most of the cases for this term were yet to be decided.

We are left with what has been written. In these final case opinions we get our final taste of Scalia's flair for the written word and the language of the law. Only the future citations know where these precedents may lead.

Bravo to Justice Scalia!
May that he rest in peace.
Long live the U.S. Supreme Court!

Long live the art of reason!

Antonin "Nino" Scalia
1936-2016

Associate Justice of the U.S. Supreme Court
1986-2016

ABOUT THE EDITOR

Joshua Warren is an artist, educator, scientist and practicing attorney with an interest in politics, language and creativity.

case law collections by this editor include:

Creativity in the Supreme Court
The U.S. Supreme Court opinions that include the word creativity

Red Herring in the Supreme Court
The U.S. Supreme Court opinions that include the phrase red herring

Alito Dissents
The U.S. Supreme Court dissenting opinions of Justice Samuel Alito

Nino's Last
The final opinions of Justice Antonin Scalia

and more...

Other artwork by Joshua Warren
can be found at:
warrbo.com

www.ingramcontent.com/pod-product-compliance
Lightning Source LLC
Chambersburg PA
CBHW020708180526
45163CB00008B/2993